Problem Solving
Book B

MW00637892

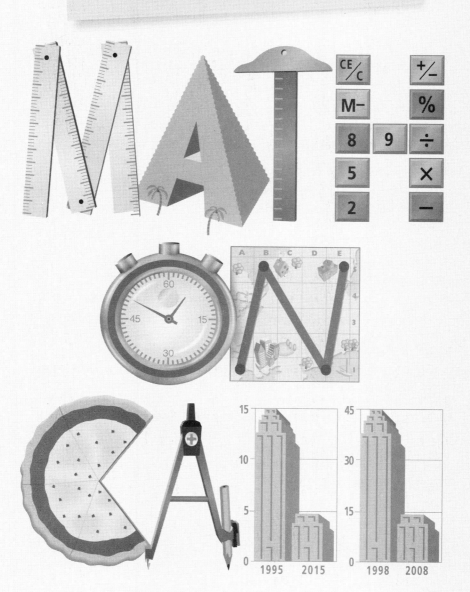

MATH ON CALL

GReaT SouRCe
EDUCATION GROUP
A Houghton Mifflin Company
New Ways to Know

Developing

thinking skills through

READING and **WRITING**

Acknowledgments

Reviewers:

Keith Case
Hoffman Middle School
Aldine ISD
Houston, TX

Stephen J. Paterwic
Mathematics Department Chair
High School of Science and Technology
Springfield, MA

Todd Stark
Shaker Heights Middle School
Shaker Heights, OH

Credits

Writing: Justine Dunn, Judy Vandegrift

Review: Ed Manfre

Editorial: Carol DeBold, Pearl Ling, Susan Rogalski

Design/Production: Taurins Design

Creative Art: Joe Boddy *page 38 (right), 54*. Alex Farquharson *pages 2, 3, 6, 19 (tree), 36, 38 (left), 40, 43, 44, 45, 46, 47, 48, 50, 55, 60, 66*. Greg Harris *pages 19 (map), 20, 22, 26, 28, 30, 42, 58, 73, 77, 104*. Eileen Hine *icons*. Stacey Schuett *pages 25, 33*.

Photos: Greg Chann *page 24*. Ron Cohn, The Gorilla Foundation/KoKo.org *page 7*. David Constantine *page 74*. Corbis *pages iv, 1 (top, bottom right), 3, 18, 19, 21, 23, 27, 29, 31, 32, 36, 37 (top), 38, 39, 40, 41, 42, 44, 48, 49, 50, 54, 55, 60, 61, 63, 69, 72, 73 (right), 77, 78, 79, 82, 90, 91, 92, 93, 97, 99*. Daniel Glenn *page 37 (bottom left)*. Library of Congress *page 37 (bottom right)*. National Geographical Society *page 51 (middle)*. National Park Service, Chaco Culture National Historical Park *page 51 (top & bottom)*. National Zoological Park *pages 1 (bottom left), 8, 11*. Royal Geographical Society *pages 73 (left & middle), 80*. Smithsonian *page 103*.

Cover Design: Kristen Davis

International Standard Book Number: 0-669-50052-6

3 4 5 6 7 8 9 –POO– 10 09 08 07 06 05

Visit our web site: http://www.greatsource.com

Table of Contents

Chapter 1

The Great Apes

Reading Piece by Piece

Dear _____,
(Your Name)

My name is Maria Lee. I'm enclosing a photograph of me from a costume party when I dressed up as a gorilla. I find gorillas and other apes fascinating.

I've spent a lot of time learning about apes. I'm especially interested in how they communicate with each other. Now I am creating a website called Great Apes. I've heard you're going to be learning about Great Apes. I'd love to hear any interesting facts or stories that you find. I want the website to be filled with interesting information.

Thanks very much. I look forward to hearing from you.

Sincerely,
Maria Lee

Maria Lee

In this chapter, you will learn about members of the Great Ape family: gorillas, chimpanzees, bonobos (pygmy chimps), and orangutans. You'll learn many facts, including some of the interesting ways these animals communicate. You'll also see the importance of communication in mathematics. Pay careful attention to words, phrases, sentences, and symbols, while you get plenty of practice using the first step of the four-step problem-solving method: **Understand.**

▼ One day in 1996 a little boy fell into the gorilla exhibit at the Brookfield Zoo. Binti Jua, a female gorilla, gently picked up the unconscious boy and brought him to the keeper's door to rescue workers. The little boy quickly recovered from his minor injuries.

◀ Washington, D.C.'s Smithsonian National Zoological Park (SNZP) has a Think Tank near the Ape House. In the Think Tank, orangutans play interactive games on a computer. One of the orangutans likes it so much that she has made the Think Tank her permanent home.

▼ Bonobos are also called pygmy chimpanzees. Their habitat is shrinking and some researchers believe there are fewer than 20,000 left.

▼ Chimpanzees learn how to make nests by watching their mothers. At first they play at making nests. Eventually, they make their own nests to sleep in.

1

Sometimes the same word can mean different things.

Often, the math meaning of a word isn't exactly the same as the everyday meaning of the word. You can get an idea about the meaning of a word by looking at how it is used.

Look at two ways the word *expression* can be used.

The *expression* on a chimpanzee's face may show how the chimp feels or what it is thinking.

Relaxed   Distressed   Playful

John used the *expression* 2*n* + 1 to represent any odd number when *n* is a whole number. ◀ MOC 204

For exercises 1–5, use the same word to complete each of the two sentences.

1. **a.** Orangutans, chimpanzees, bonobos, and gorillas are all part of the

    Great Ape family. One thing these species have in _____ is
    that they all use tools.

   b. In a _____ fraction, the numerator and denominator are both
    whole numbers. ◀ MOC 576

   MATH ON CALL

   This number tells you where to find more information in *Math on Call*.

   Look for the vocabulary words on this page. Circle them. Then go to the Vocabulary section, which begins on page 108. Write definitions for the words. Include diagrams and/or examples.

Vocabulary ▼ expression ▼ odd number ▼ whole number ▼ numerator ▼ denominator

2. a. Orangutans are endangered because their _____ habitat, the forest, is being destroyed.

   b. The numbers 1, 2, 3, 4, and so on are called counting numbers or _____ numbers. ◂MOC 585

3. a. The pictures below show how a chimp's hand and foot are _____ to a human's hand and foot.

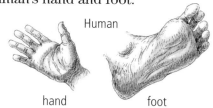
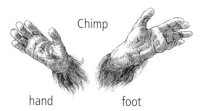

Human   hand   foot   Chimp   hand   foot

   b. The 6-inch square and 3-inch square are _____ to each other, but not to the other rectangle. ◂MOC 376

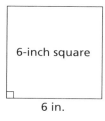
6-inch square
6 in.

3-inch square
3 in.

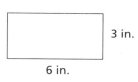
3 in.
6 in.

4. a. Some movies make people develop a _____ attitude toward gorillas. The movie *King Kong* made many people believe that gorillas are ferocious.

   b. Numbers less than zero are called _____ numbers. ◂MOC 046

5. a. Gorillas eat only plants. They use their powerful teeth to cut and grind the stalk, shoot, and _____ of a plant.

   b. The square _____ of 9 is $^+3$ or $^-3$. ◂MOC 076–077

The Great Apes

Bonobo

Gorilla

Chimpanzee

Orangutan

more ▸

Vocabulary ▧ counting numbers ▧ square

Now you'll write your own sentences to show different meanings of the same word.

Write one sentence that shows an everyday meaning of the word and one sentence that shows the math meaning of the word.

6. power ◀MOC 071

_____

_____

7. origin ◀MOC 318

_____

_____

8. regular ◀MOC 590

_____

_____

9. mean ◀MOC 274

_____

_____

10. leg ◀MOC 358

_____

_____

11. function ◀MOC 234

_____

_____

12. operation ◂MOC 586

_____

_____

_____

13. ray ◂MOC 322

_____

_____

_____

14. prime ◂MOC 058

_____

_____

_____

15. range ◂MOC 272

_____

_____

_____

16. chord ◂MOC 370

_____

_____

_____

17. net ◂MOC 395

_____

_____

_____

more ▸

Sometimes different words can mean the same thing.

Chimpanzees have different facial expressions that show fear.

In math, we often have several different ways to say or write the same thing. Look at this sentence.

The average adult chimpanzee is <u>33 inches</u> long.

There are many other ways to name the underlined measure without changing the meaning of the sentence. Here are some examples:

- thirty-three inches
- 33 in.
- 33"

- 2 feet 9 inches
- $2\frac{3}{4}$ feet
- 2.75 feet

Circle the words or numbers that mean the same as the underlined part of the sentence. Circle as many as you can.

18. Gorillas have long arms and short legs. One male gorilla had an arm span that measured <u>9 feet 2 inches</u>. ◀MOC 536

$9\frac{1}{6}$ feet	110 inches	92 inches
9' 2"	9" 2'	9.2 feet

19. Gorillas can live <u>up to 50</u> years.

more than 50	as many as 50	longer than 50
50 or more	about 50	a maximum of 50

20. Koko, a gorilla, can communicate using American Sign Language. She knows <u>more than 1000</u> words.

over 1000	more than 10^3	more than a thousand
less than 1000	under 1000	more than a million

21. Gorillas sleep <u>about 13</u> hours each night.

approximately 13	13 or more	close to 13
around 13	more than 13	less than 13

Write two other ways to say or write the underlined part of the sentence.

22. Gorillas usually move slowly, but if they have to run fast, they can run
    <u>20 miles per hour</u>.

    _____   _____

23. Mountain gorillas are a subspecies of gorillas. Males generally weigh <u>less than 500</u>
    pounds.

    _____   _____

24. Chimps can cover <u>as many as 4 miles a day</u> in search of food.

    _____   _____

25. A chimp can pull a load of <u>more than 800</u> pounds with only one hand.

    _____   _____

26. Research shows that chimpanzees and humans share <u>about 98 percent</u> of the
    same genes. ◂ MOC 442

    _____   _____

▪◪▪▪◪◪▪◪▪◪▪◪◪◪
Koko is a mountain gorilla who has learned
sign language. Here, she signs *sorry*.

Vocabulary ◪ miles per hour (mph) ◪ fewer ◪ percent (%)

Sometimes, you need to make a sketch of what you read.

When you draw a diagram to help you solve a math problem, the picture will be very simple. It should just show the details that represent the math.

Kojo, Ktembe, and Kwame are three young male gorillas that were born and live at the National Zoological Park in Washington, D.C. Ktembe is 2 years older than Kwame and Kojo is 2 years younger than Kwame.

Kojo Ktembe Kwame

When you draw a diagram to show the math from the sentences above, you don't need to draw pictures of gorillas. You can use a number line to show the relationships between their ages.

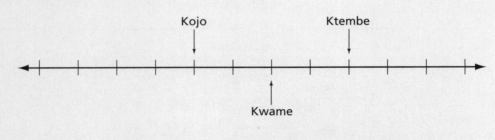

In front of exercises 1–5, write the letter of the diagram that best shows the relationships.

_____ 1. Haloko, Kigali, and Mandara are three female gorillas living at the National Zoological Park. Haloko is 15 years older than Mandara and Kigali is 12 years younger than Mandara.

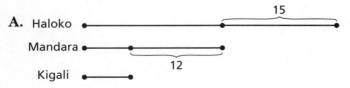 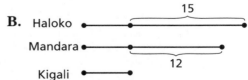

8

_____ **2.** Ktembe is a young male mountain gorilla who weighs twice as much as his half-brother, Kwame.

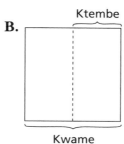

A. Kwame / Ktembe

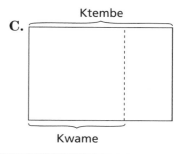

B. Ktembe / Kwame

C. Ktembe / Kwame

_____ **3.** All orangutans are great apes, but all great apes are not orangutans. ◀MOC 594

A. Orangutans   Great Apes

B. Orangutans / Great Apes

C. Great Apes / Orangutans

_____ **4.** Western gorillas eat about 5 times as many species of plants as do mountain gorillas.

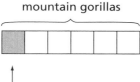

A. mountain gorillas / western gorillas

B. western gorillas / mountain gorillas

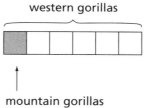

C. western gorillas / mountain gorillas

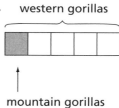

_____ **5.** At Zoo Atlanta, one group of gorillas eats $\frac{2}{3}$ as much fruit as vegetables.

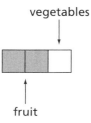

A. vegetables / fruit

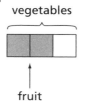

B. vegetables / fruit

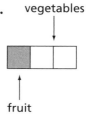

C. vegetables / fruit

more ▶

Make sure that your drawings match the math.

Cross out the diagram or diagrams that do *not* show the math.

6. Gorillas and chimps are part of the Great Ape family, but monkeys are not. ◀MOC 594

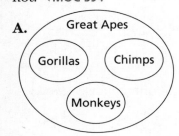
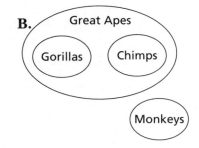
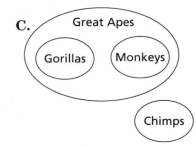

7. Azy, Bonnie, and Kiko are orangutans living at the Smithsonian National Zoological Park. Kiko weighs 17 kilograms more than Bonnie does. Azy weighs 28 kilograms more than Kiko does.

A. Bonnie
Kiko 17
Azy 17 28

B. Bonnie
Kiko 17
Azy 28

C. Kiko 17
Bonnie
Azy 17 28

8. In the open woods where there are few trees, chimpanzees need to cover a greater area to find food. During a single year, a group of chimps might wander over an area of a hundred square miles. ◀MOC 347

A.
100 miles (top)
100 miles (left) · 100 miles (right)
100 miles (bottom)

B.
10 miles (top)
10 miles (left) · 10 miles (right)
10 miles (bottom)

9. There are 3 subspecies of gorillas: western gorillas, eastern gorillas, and mountain gorillas. ◀MOC 364

A. Gorillas
western gorillas | eastern gorillas | mountain gorillas

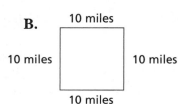
B. Gorillas — Western, Eastern, Mountain

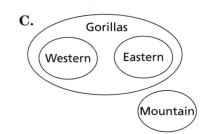
C. Gorillas — Western, Eastern, Mountain

Draw a diagram to represent the math.

10. The mean height of adult female gorillas standing on 2 legs is about 90% of that of adult males. ◀MOC 274, 442

11. A gorilla ate 50 pounds of food each day for a week.

12. There are about $\frac{1}{4}$ as many mountain gorillas as eastern gorillas left in the wild. ◀MOC 028

13. The great apes and humans are both primates. ◀MOC 364

14. The O Line has eight 10-foot towers that support plastic-covered steel cables.

Many of the orangutans at the National Zoological Park travel along a 400-foot *O Line* to get from the Great Ape House to the Think Tank.

symbol represents a word or group of words.

According to their trainers, some bonobos, or pygmy chimps, have learned to understand English and to reply to questions or ask for things by pointing to symbols. Here are a few symbols from the bonobos' vocabulary.

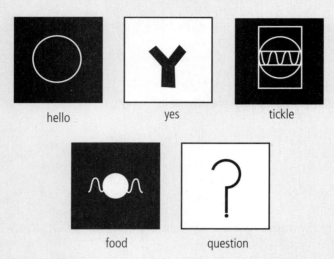

hello   yes   tickle

food   question

Mathematics uses symbols, too. We often use symbols to represent quantities and operations. Here are some examples.

$+$	$-$	$\times$	$\div$	π
plus	minus	times	divided by	the ratio of C to d in a circle

Letters are also used as symbols in the language of mathematics. A letter can be used to represent a number that is not known, or a value that changes. When letters are used in this way, they are called *variables*.

We often use variables to show how unknown or changing quantities are related. Consider this statement.

> **The human brain is larger than the ape brain. The average volume for a human brain is 3 times the volume of the largest ape brain.**

- Suppose we let a stand for the volume in cubic inches of the largest ape brain. Then $3 \times a$ or $3a$ can be used to represent the average volume in cubic inches of a human brain.

- Suppose we let h stand for the average volume in cubic inches of a human brain. Then $h \div 3$ or $\frac{h}{3}$ can be used to represent the volume in cubic inches of the largest ape brain.

Circle the correct expression. ◀MOC 200–204

1. The mean weight of a male orangutan is 70 pounds more than the mean weight of a female orangutan. ◀MOC 274

   a. Suppose you let x stand for the mean weight in pounds of a female orangutan. Which expression can be used to represent the mean weight in pounds of a male orangutan?

   $x + 70$ $\qquad\qquad$ $x - 70$ $\qquad\qquad$ $70x$ $\qquad\qquad$ $\frac{x}{70}$

   b. Suppose you let y stand for the mean weight in pounds of a male orangutan. Which expression can be used to represent the mean weight in pounds of a female orangutan?

   $y + 70$ $\qquad\qquad$ $y - 70$ $\qquad\qquad$ $70y$ $\qquad\qquad$ $\frac{y}{70}$

2. The mean length of a female orangutan is $\frac{3}{4}$ of the mean length of a male orangutan. ◀MOC 187, 189

   a. If you let x stand for the mean length in inches of a male orangutan, which expression represents the mean length in inches of a female orangutan?

   $x + \frac{3}{4}$ $\qquad\qquad$ $x - \frac{3}{4}$ $\qquad\qquad$ $\frac{3}{4}x$ $\qquad\qquad$ $x \div \frac{3}{4}$

   b. If you let y stand for the mean length in inches of a female orangutan, which expression represents the mean length in inches of a male orangutan? ◀MOC 187, 189

   $y + \frac{3}{4}$ $\qquad\qquad$ $y - \frac{3}{4}$ $\qquad\qquad$ $\frac{3}{4}y$ $\qquad\qquad$ $\frac{4}{3}y$

3. A kilogram is equivalent to about 2.2 pounds.

   a. If you let x stand for the mean weight in *pounds* of a male orangutan, which expression represents the approximate mean weight in *kilograms* of a male orangutan?

   $x + 2.2$ $\qquad\qquad$ $x - 2.2$ $\qquad\qquad$ $2.2x$ $\qquad\qquad$ $\frac{x}{2.2}$

   b. If you let y stand for the mean weight in *kilograms* of a male orangutan, which expression represents the approximate mean weight in *pounds* of a male orangutan?

   $y + 2.2$ $\qquad\qquad$ $y - 2.2$ $\qquad\qquad$ $2.2y$ $\qquad\qquad$ $\frac{y}{2.2}$

more ▶

When you write an expression, think about how the quantities are related.

Write a correct expression. ◂MOC 201–204

4. The mean weight of a male gorilla is 1.75 times the mean weight of a female gorilla.

   a. Let x stand for the mean weight in pounds of a female gorilla. Write an expression that represents the mean weight in pounds of a male gorilla.

        _____

   b. Let y stand for the mean weight in pounds of a male gorilla. Write an expression that represents the mean weight in pounds of a female gorilla.

        _____

5. The mean length of a female gorilla is 8 inches less than the mean length of a male gorilla.

   a. Let x stand for the mean length in inches of the male gorilla. Write an expression that represents the mean length in inches of a female gorilla.

        _____

   b. Let y stand for the mean length in inches of a female gorilla. Write an expression that represents the mean length in inches of a male gorilla.

        _____

6. One foot is equivalent to 12 inches.

   a. Let x stand for the mean length in *inches* of a male gorilla. Write an expression that represents the mean length in *feet* of a male gorilla.

        _____

   b. Let y stand for the mean length in *feet* of a male gorilla. Write an expression that represents the mean length in *inches* of a male gorilla.

        _____

The letter you use as a variable doesn't need to be the same one your friends use.

Choose a variable and write a correct expression.

7. The mean weight of a male gorilla is 220% of the mean weight of a male human. ◀MOC 442

   a. Choose a variable to stand for the mean weight in pounds of a male human. Write an expression that represents the mean weight in pounds of a male gorilla. (HINT: Write 220% as a decimal.)

   _____

   b. Choose a variable to stand for the mean weight in pounds of a male gorilla. Write an expression that represents the mean weight in pounds of a male human. (HINT: Write 220% as a decimal.)

   _____

8. The mean weight of a female human is 70% of the mean weight of a female gorilla. ◀MOC 442

   a. Choose a variable to stand for the mean weight in pounds of a female gorilla. Write an expression that represents the mean weight in pounds of female human. (HINT: Write 70% as a decimal.)

   _____

   b. Choose a variable to stand for the mean weight in pounds of a female human. Write an expression that represents the mean weight in pounds of female gorilla. (HINT: Write 70% as a decimal.)

   _____

9. Despite the size of adult gorillas, the mean weight of a newborn gorilla is half the mean weight of a newborn human.

   a. Choose a variable to stand for the mean weight in pounds of a newborn gorilla. Write an expression that represents the mean weight in pounds of a newborn human.

   _____

   b. Choose a variable to stand for the mean weight in pounds of a newborn human. Write an expression that represents the mean weight in pounds of a newborn gorilla.

   _____

15

Write the same word to make both sentences true.

1. **a.** The _____ on Mom's face showed that she was upset.

   b. A mathematical _____ may contain a number, a variable, and an operation sign.

2. **a.** Rick fell off the horse and broke his _____.

   b. Each of the two shorter sides of a right triangle is called a _____.

For exercises 3–5, mark the letter of the phrase or number that means the same as the underlined part of the sentence.

3. <u>Around 30</u> people came to the party.

   A Exactly 30

   B Almost 30

   C Approximately 30

   D Thirty or more

4. The bus was traveling at 50 <u>miles per hour</u>.

   A mph

   B mhp

   C miles

   D hours

5. Christina is <u>4' 3"</u> tall.

   A $4\frac{1}{3}$ feet

   B 4 feet 3 inches

   C 4.3 feet

   D 4 inches 3 feet

For exercises 6–7, draw a diagram that shows the mathematical relationship.

6. Janine is 4 inches shorter than Brett. Fran is 5 inches taller than Brett.

7. Lettuce and spinach are vegetables, but tomatoes are not.

Write a correct expression.

8. Harriet is 4 years older than Catherine. Suppose x stands for Catherine's age. Write an expression that represents Harriet's age.

_____

9. Frisky and Sunshine are cats. Frisky weighs twice as much as Sunshine. Suppose y stands for Sunshine's weight. Write an expression that stands for Frisky's weight.

_____

Write your response on the lines provided. You may wish to draw a diagram.

10. Write two sentences to show the difference between the way we use the word *regular* in everyday life and the way we use the word *regular* in geometry.

_____

_____

_____

_____

17

A Visit to Brazil

Finding Exactly What You Need

| Send To | Attachments |

TO _____
(Your Name)

From: linda@travel.gsps

subject : Travel Poster for Brazil

We would like you to create a travel poster for the country of Brazil. Brazil is an amazing country with everything from big cities to rain forests. We'd like the poster to show all of the variety that Brazil has to offer.

We have arranged for you to take a tour of Brazil before you create the poster. In each place you visit, a young person about your age will greet you and show you around.

In this chapter, you will be learning about Brazil. You'll find out that Brazil has something for everyone. As you visit a tropical rain forest and beautiful beaches, you'll find out about the greatest soccer player of all time. While you practice finding information that is shown in tables and graphs, you'll also learn how to find just the information you need in order to solve a math problem. This will help you with the first step of the Problem-Solving method: **Understand**.

Brazil

▼ Brazilian Portuguese is different from the Portuguese spoken in Portugal. This is because Brazilian Portuguese has been influenced by the native language group called *Tupi-Guarani*. The Portuguese used *Tupi* and *Guarani* words to name unfamiliar animals and plants. Some of these words, like *jaguar*, are now also used in the English language.

▲ Brazil got its name from a wood called *pau brazil* or *pernambuco*. This wood was important because red dye was extracted from it until about 1850. It has also been used in the manufacture of violin bows since the mid-1700s, but it is listed as an endangered species in Brazil today.

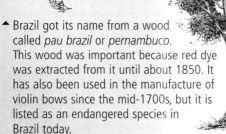

▼ The trees in the rain forest of Brazil can grow as high as 165 feet.

▲ The most famous soccer player the world has ever known was born in Brazil. His name is Pelé. Pelé began his career in soccer playing soccer in the streets of Brazil with a ball made out of old socks.

19

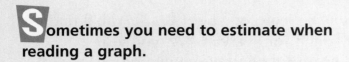

Sometimes you need to estimate when reading a graph.

The first person you meet on the tour is Juliana. She lives in Brasilia, the capital city of Brazil. Her father works for the Brazilian government.

Juliana tells you some facts about Brazil and shows you 2 bar graphs and a circle graph.

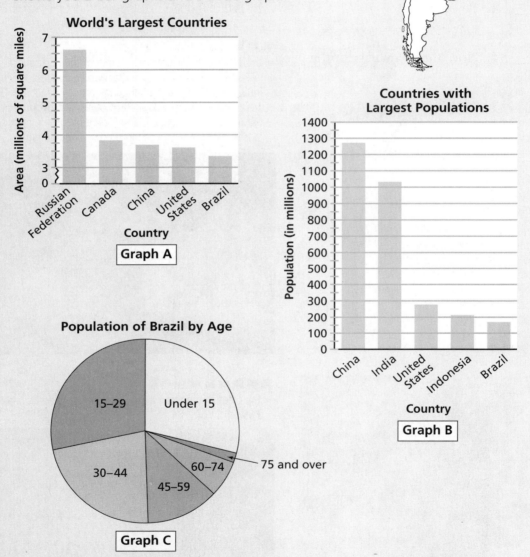

You realize that, when reading the graphs, you will need to use your estimation skills. The graphs don't give you exact numbers, but they still show plenty of information.

Vocabulary ▼ bar graph ▼ circle graph ▼ estimation

Study the graphs on page 20. Tell whether the statement is true or false. Then circle the letter of the graph you used to decide. ◀MOC 287–292, 296

_____ 1. Brazil is the smallest country in the world.   **A   B   C**

_____ 2. Brazil is the fifth largest country in the world.   **A   B   C**

_____ 3. The population of Brazil is between 100,000,000 and 200,000,000.   **A   B   C**

_____ 4. More than a quarter of the people in Brazil are under 15 years old. **A   B   C**

_____ 5. The area of Brazil is more than 3,000,000 square miles.   **A   B   C**

_____ 6. The population of Brazil is greater than that of the U. S.   **A   B   C**

_____ 7. The population of China is more than 1 billion.   **A   B   C**

_____ 8. Less than half of the population of Brazil is under 30 years old.   **A   B   C**

_____ 9. The Russian Federation is more than twice as large as Canada.   **A   B   C**

_____ 10. Brazil is smaller than the United States.   **A   B   C**

Brasilia is a planned city. Construction began in 1956, so the city is an example of 20th century architecture and city planning. Many people find the modern buildings and impressive monuments fascinating. Some people, however, dislike the city because it is divided into many sections with specific purposes, such as hotels and banking.

more ▶

Vocabulary ◢ area

Line graphs are useful for showing change over time.

Next, you meet Paulo, who lives in the city of Rio de Janeiro. Many people think that Rio de Janeiro is the most beautiful city on earth. It has beautiful beaches, mountains, palm trees, tropical flowers, birds, and butterflies. Paulo's family lives in a house on the hillside.

Paulo tells you about the city's wonderful climate and shows you these line graphs so you can see the average monthly temperature and the average monthly rainfall.

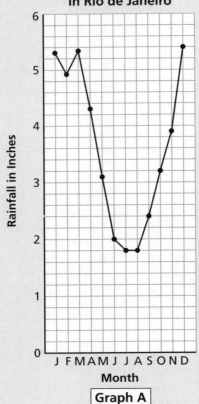

Average Monthly Rainfall in Rio de Janeiro

Graph A

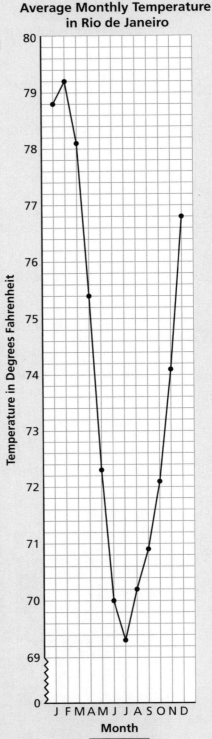

Average Monthly Temperature in Rio de Janeiro

Graph B

22

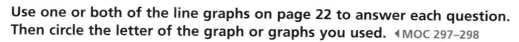

Use one or both of the line graphs on page 22 to answer each question. Then circle the letter of the graph or graphs you used. ◂MOC 297–298

11. What is the highest monthly average temperature?

_____   A   B

12. What is the lowest monthly average temperature?

_____   A   B

13. Which months have the least rainfall?

_____   A   B

14. Which month has the most rainfall?

_____   A   B

15. How much rain falls in the warmest month?

_____   A   B

16. What is the average rainfall in October?

_____   A   B

17. What is the average temperature in May?

_____   A   B

18. What is the average temperature in the wettest month?

_____   A   B

Did you know?
Rio de Janeiro's most famous and beautiful beach is Copacabana. There are 25,000 people per square kilometer living there. This is one of the most crowded areas of the world.

Write the answer to question 19 on the lines provided.

19. In what month would you like to visit Rio de Janeiro? Explain your thinking.

_____

_____

_____

_____

_____

more ▸

Vocabulary ▾ line graph ▾ square kilometer (km²)

Graphs and equations can show the relationship between two variables.

In Brazil, the unit of currency is the *real*.

The relationship between units of currency from different countries can change from day to day. Paulo's sister, Maria, makes a table that shows the relationship between U. S. dollars and Brazilian reais for the day you are visiting Rio de Janeiro.

U. S. Dollars	Brazilian Reais
1	2.95
2	5.90
3	8.85

Use the table above to answer these questions.

20. Circle the letter of the graph that shows the relationship shown in the table. ◀MOC 232–234

A.

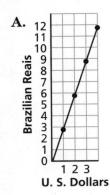

B.

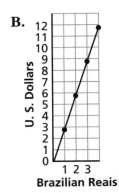

21. Let d represent the number of U. S. dollars and let r represent the number of Brazilian reais. Circle the equation that shows the relationship shown in the table. ◀MOC 244

Equation A: $r = 2.95d$ **Equation B:** $d = 2.95r$

24   Vocabulary ▼ table ▼ equation

Maria takes you to the beach where you meet Francisco, who is selling hats. The graph shows the cost of the hats.

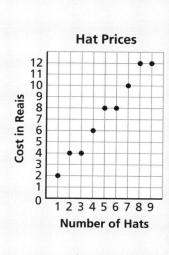

Hat Prices

Use the graph above to answer the questions. ◂MOC 234

22. What is the cost of 2 hats? _____

23. How much will you pay for 6 hats? _____

24. How many hats can you buy with 4 reais? _____

25. Use the graph you chose in exercise 20. Estimate the cost in U. S. dollars of 3 hats.

_____

26. Use words to describe the cost of the hats. _____

_____

27. Why do you think the points on the graph are not connected by line segments? ◂MOC 235

_____

_____

more ▸

When you take a survey, there are many ways to show the results.

You travel to Bahia to meet Danusha, who lives in the city of Salvador. She takes you to some street-side food stands, where all of the members of your group get to try four different dishes. All of these dishes reflect the African and Portuguese traditions of Bahia.

You take a survey of the people in your group. Each person votes for the one food he or she liked best. You show the results in a table.

Food from Bahia	Number of People Who Like It Best
Feijoada, the national dish of Brazil, a black bean and pork stew	ℍℍ ℍℍ
Vatapá, a spicy shrimp dish	ℍℍ ℍℍ ℍℍ ℍℍ
Moqueca, a dish made with vegetables and shrimp and coconut	ℍℍ //
Acarajé, a fried food made from black-eyed peas	ℍℍ ℍℍ ///

Use the table to answer these questions. ◄ MOC 264, 269

28. How many of the people chose Vatapá? _____

29. How many people voted in the survey? _____

30. What fraction of the people chose Vatapá? ◄ MOC 028 _____

31. What percent of the people chose Moqueca? ◄ MOC 442 _____

32. Complete this bar graph so that it shows the same information as the table. ◄ MOC 292

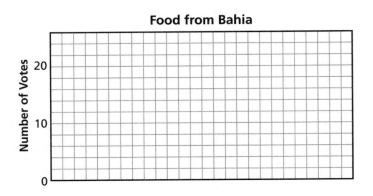

Food from Bahia

Number of Votes

Food

33. Which of these circle graphs shows the same information as the table on page 26? ◀ MOC 296, 442

A. Favorite Bahian Food

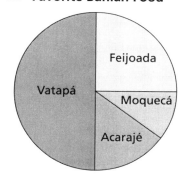

C. Favorite Bahian Food

B. Favorite Bahian Food

D. Favorite Bahian Food

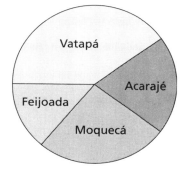

34. Explain how you made your choice in exercise 33.

_____
_____
_____
_____
_____
_____
_____
_____

Ver-O-Peso Market in Belem

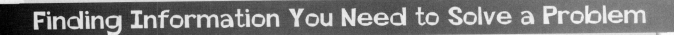

Some problems give you more information than you need.

Soccer, called *futebol* in Brazil, is a national pastime. You meet Danilo, who loves to play the game and tells you some facts about soccer in Brazil.

Danilo is proud of the fact that he lives in Três Corações because that is the birthplace of Pelé, considered by many to be the best soccer player of all time.

Três Corações

Place a check next to the fact or facts you could use to solve each problem.

1. How many times has Brazil won the World Cup?

   ☐ Since 1930, the World Cup soccer tournament has been played every four years. Teams who qualify from all over the world participate.

   ☐ Brazil won the World Cup in 1958, 1962, 1970, 1994, and 2002.

2. During the World Cup finals in 1950, how many seats in Maracanã Stadium were empty? ◀MOC 129

   ☐ The record attendance at the Maracanã Stadium was 199,854 people for the World Cup finals in 1950.

   ☐ Until 1998, the Maracanã Stadium in Rio de Janeiro was the largest soccer stadium in the world and could seat 200,000 people.

   ☐ In 1998, much of the Maracanã Stadium was declared unusable because of its poor condition. Its current capacity is 70,000.

3. How old was Pelé when he played his first World Cup game?

   ☐ Edson Arantes do Nascimento, nicknamed Pelé, was born on October 23, 1940.

   ☐ During his first World Cup tournament, Pelé scored 6 goals.

   ☐ Pelé played his first World Cup game in June of 1958.

4. How many goals per game did Pelé average during his career? ◀ MOC 274

☐ Pelé scored 1281 goals during his career.

☐ During his first World Cup tournament, Pelé scored 6 goals.

☐ Pelé played 1363 games during his career.

5. How old was Pelé when he scored his 1000th goal?

☐ Pelé scored his 1000th goal in Maracanã Stadium.

☐ Edson Arantes do Nascimento, nicknamed Pelé, was born on October 23, 1940.

☐ Pelé scored his 1000th goal on November 19, 1969.

6. In what percent of his games did Pelé score at least 3 goals? ◀ MOC 444

☐ Pelé scored 1281 goals during his career.

☐ Pelé scored 5 goals in a game on 6 occasions, 4 goals on 30 occasions, and a hat-trick (3 goals) on 92 occasions.

☐ Pelé played 1363 games during his career.

☐ Pelé scored his 1000th goal on November 19, 1969 in Maracanã Stadium.

Pelé was known for his killer instinct in front of the goal, an eye for the perfect pass, and his incredible dribbling skills. He had it all: technique, speed, and intelligence.

Sometimes a problem doesn't give you all the information you need to solve it.

For some problems, when information is missing, you can find that information yourself. For example, you might need to know the formula for the volume of a cube or the number of inches in a cubit. Sometimes you can find the information in an almanac or other reference material.

Rain Forest

However, for some problems, you won't be able to solve the problem until someone gives you the information that is missing.

The next stop on the trip is the rain forest of northwestern Brazil. You meet Olavo. He does not go to school because there are no schools where he lives. He works with his father who is a *seringueriro*, a rubber tapper. Olavo's father's job is to collect white sap, or latex, from wild rubber trees. Olavo tells you about the rain forest.

Read each problem. Then answer the questions.

1. The tropical rain forest takes up more than half of the area of Brazil and it is nine times the size of Texas. What is the area of Brazil's rain forest in square miles? ◄MOC 347

   a. Is any information missing from the problem? If *yes*, tell what information is missing and answer question b.

   _____

   b. Can you find the missing information? If *yes*, write the information and tell how you found it.

   _____

   _____

30

2. The rain forest gets about 160 inches of rain each year. Would that much rain fill a bucket as tall as your classroom?

   a. Is any information missing from the problem? If *yes*, tell what information is missing and answer question b.

   _____

   b. Can you find the missing information? If *yes*, write the information and tell how you found it.

   _____

   _____

3. One third of the world's rain forests are located in Brazil. What percent of the world's rain forests are located in Brazil? ◀ MOC 442–443

   a. Is any information missing from the problem? If *yes*, tell what information is missing and answer question b.

   _____

   _____

   b. Can you find the missing information? If *yes*, write the information and tell how you found it.

   _____

   _____

   _____

   _____

Did you know?
Rain forests are very important. They act like huge sponges that hold water and release it slowly. They provide one fifth of the world's people with fresh drinking water and help prevent soil from being washed away. In addition, many medicines are made using plants from the rain forest. For example, the rosy periwinkle is used to make medicine to help children with leukemia, a cancer of the blood.

more ▶

Sometimes you can find the information that is missing, but sometimes you can't.

4. Olavo's father has made two trails so that he can collect latex from the rubber trees. One trail connects 119 rubber trees. It takes Olavo's father seven hours to tap all of the trees on the trail. About how many trees can he tap in an hour? ◄MOC 179

   a. Is any information missing from the problem? If *yes*, tell what information is missing and answer question b.

   _____

   b. Can you find the missing information? If *yes*, write the information and tell how you found it.

   _____

   _____

5. Olavo's father can fill 3 identical pails ($4\frac{1}{2}$ gallons in all) with latex from the trees on the trail. How many quarts of latex does each pail hold? ◄MOC 536

   a. Is any information missing from the problem? If *yes*, tell what information is missing and answer question b.

   _____

   b. Can you find the missing information? If *yes*, write the information and tell how you found it.

   _____

   _____

   _____

   _____

   _____

A rubber tapper first scrapes away the rough top layer of bark. Then, after three or four days, he makes a diagonal cut in the bark. The groove fills with latex. He uses a small cup to catch the latex.

6. After collecting the latex, Olavo's father uses special smoke to turn the latex into solid rubber. It takes about 26 gallons of latex to make a rubber ball large enough to sell. If he sells 2 balls during one month, how much money will he receive?

a. Is any information missing from the problem? If *yes*, tell what information is missing and answer question b.

_____

_____

b. Can you find the missing information? If *yes*, write the information and tell how you found it.

_____

_____

7. In some areas, rain forests are being destroyed at a rate of 50 acres per minute. How many square miles per day is that? ◂MOC 536

a. Is any information missing from the problem? If *yes*, tell what information is missing and answer question b.

_____

_____

b. Can you find the missing information? If *yes*, write the information and tell how you found it.

_____

_____

_____

Olavo explains that products such as Brazil nuts and latex are kind to the rain forest because they don't destroy the trees.

You think about this as you travel home with memories of the beautiful country of Brazil and its wonderful people. You have lots of ideas for the travel poster and can't wait to get started.

Vocabulary ▸ acre

Fill in the circle with the letter of the correct answer.

1. According to the bar graph, which of these statements is true?

   (A) Mount Everest is a little more than 29 feet high.

   (B) K2 is between 28,200 and 28,400 feet high.

   (C) Makalu is between 27,080 and 27,090 feet high.

   (D) Makalu is the world's third-highest mountain.

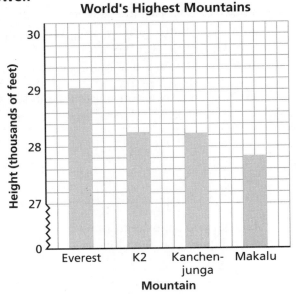

World's Highest Mountains

2. According to the line graph, which is Boston's coldest month?

   (A) December

   (B) January

   (C) February

   (D) None of these

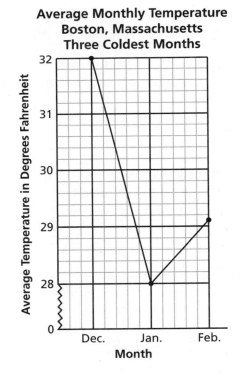

Average Monthly Temperature Boston, Massachusetts Three Coldest Months

3. According to the line graph, what is the average monthly temperature in Boston in February?

   (A) 30°F

   (B) 29.1°F

   (C) 29.5°F

   (D) 29°F

34

 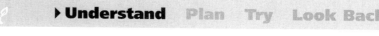

For exercise 4, fill in the circle with the letter of the correct graph and explain why you made your choice.

4. Stop & Save sells American cheese for $3.00 per pound. Which graph shows the relationship between the amount of cheese you buy and the total cost?

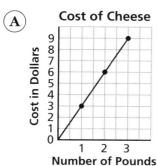

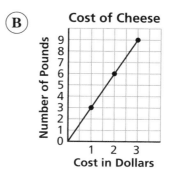

_____

_____

_____

For exercises 5–7, write your answer on the lines provided.

5. Every day of this week, Andrew ran for 45 minutes. What information could you use to find out how far Andrew ran this week?

_____

_____

6. Twenty-five percent of the girls and thirty percent of the boys from Ms. DeLima's class play basketball after school. What information could you use to find the number of boys from Ms De Lima's class who play basketball after school?

_____

7. Study the circle graph. Write three things the graph shows.

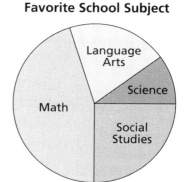

Favorite School Subject

_____

_____

_____

_____

EXPO OF THE AMERICAS

Making a Plan

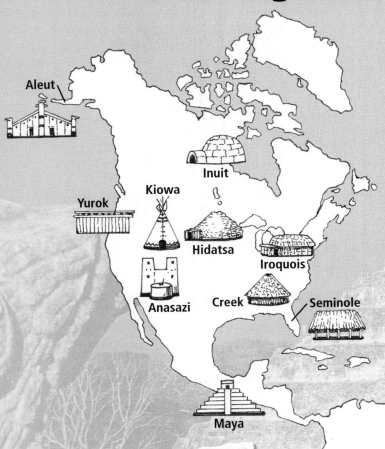

Aleut

Inuit

Kiowa

Yurok

Hidatsa

Iroquois

Anasazi

Creek

Seminole

Maya

Inca

HELP WANTED

Assistant to architect designing Native American Architecture exhibit

Must have knowledge of Native American architecture, good problem-solving skills, and love of travel. Send letter expressing your interest to Onatah Wanyandie.

36

In this chapter, you'll learn about the planning that goes into building homes and other structures. You'll also learn how to make a plan to solve a math problem. You will get plenty of practice using the first and second steps in the four-step problem-solving method: **Understand** and **Plan**.

▼ Igloos were used as temporary shelters by the Inuit.

◀ Native American dwellings were often heated with a central fire. Several tribal groups used tipis as either permanent or temporary housing.

▶ Native Americans had to insulate their houses to protect themselves from extreme temperatures. This Aleut house has double walls filled with grass.

▼ Daniel Glenn is a Crow architect who helped design these buildings at Little Big Horn College on the Crow Reservation in southern Montana. He combines traditional and modern ideas in his work.

▲ This Seminole house has open sides and a raised sleeping platform to allow air to flow easily throughout the living space in their hot climate.

Seeing how the parts of a problem go together is the key to a good plan.

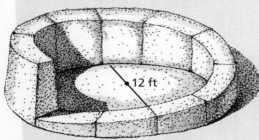

12 ft

Congratulations! I am Onatah Wanyandie and I have chosen you to be my assistant. We are going to create a village to show the architecture of different Native American cultures. I want you to travel throughout North and South America to see for yourself the types of buildings we will construct for the village. You will see that, to make a plan for a structure, you need to know how the pieces are related—how they fit together. You will also decide how the parts of math problems are related in order to make plans to solve them.

You will first go to the arctic to look at igloos.

To show how the parts of the problem are related, complete each sentence with words or numbers from the box.

1. You send a diagram to Ms Wanyandie to give her an idea of the size of the blocks of ice. How long is each block of ice in the bottom row of the igloo? ◀MOC 372

   a. The length of a block equals the length of the entire

   row _____ the number of blocks.

multiplied by
divided by

   b. The bottom row has _____ blocks arranged

   in a rough _____.

10	rectangle
π	circle
5	

   c. The length of the entire bottom row is about the same as the

   _____ of a 12-foot circle.

radius
diameter
circumference

   d. The circumference of a circle equals the length

   of its _____ times _____.

radius	π
diameter	2
circumference	3

Vocabulary ▼ rectangle ▼ circle ▼ radius ▼ diameter ▼ circumference ▼ pi (π)

You are amazed to see that an igloo can be built in a few hours.

Did you know?
The igloo builder has to find just the right kind of snow. If it is too hard, a knife won't cut it and if it is too soft, the blocks will fall apart.

2. A block of ice is 3 feet 2 inches long, $1\frac{1}{2}$ feet wide, and 6 inches high. What is the volume of the block in cubic inches? ◀MOC 402, 536

> cylinder
> rectangular prism
> square

   a. The block is in the shape of a _____.

> sum   quotient
> difference   width
> product   weight

   b. The volume of the block is the _____ of

   the length, _____, and height of the block.

> the same as
> less than
> greater than

   c. The block of ice is 3 feet 2 inches long.

   This is _____ 38 inches.

> 1.5
> 12
> 18

   d. The block of ice is $1\frac{1}{2}$ feet or _____ inches wide.

3. A block of ice has a volume of 4100 cubic inches. Ice weighs 0.53 ounces per cubic inch. How many pounds does the block weigh? ◀MOC 536

> added to
> subtracted from
> multiplied by
> divided by

   a. The weight of the block of ice in ounces is equal to 0.53

   _____ 4100.

> added to
> subtracted from
> multiplied by
> divided by

   b. The weight in pounds is equal to the number

   of ounces _____ 16.

more ▶

Vocabulary ▾ cylinder ▾ rectangular prism ▾ sum ▾ difference ▾ product ▾ quotient

39

Formulas and other equations can help you show how parts of a problem are related.

You're ready for some warmer weather so you travel to Mexico to learn about the architecture of the Maya civilization.

To show how the parts of the problem are related, complete each sentence with words or numbers from the box.

4. You notice that the faces at the ends of the roofs are isosceles triangles. If m∠A is 65°, what is m∠C? ◀MOC 351

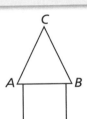

a. The base angles of an isosceles triangle are _____.

Since m∠A = _____ then m∠B = _____.

similar	65°
congruent	180°
supplementary	25°
90°	

b. The measure of any angle of a triangle is equal to

180° _____ the _____ of the measures of the other two angles.

plus	sum
minus	difference
times	

c. The measures of the angles of a triangle have

a sum of _____.

That means _____ = 180°.

90°	m∠A + m∠B
180°	ABC
m∠A + m∠B + m∠C	

180° + (65° + 65°)
180° − 2(65°)
180° × 65°
90° − 2(65°)

d. So, m∠C = _____.

40   Vocabulary ▼ isosceles ▼ similar ▼ congruent ▼ supplementary angle

5. You need to figure out the cost of buying materials to construct the roof of a Maya house. To do that, you'll need to know the area of the roof. What is the area of the front face of the roof of the Maya house? ◀MOC 368

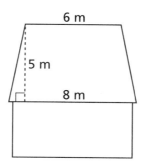

6 m

5 m

8 m

a. The front of the roof is a _____.

triangle
rectangle
circle
trapezoid

b. Area of front of roof = _____

= _____

ℓw	6×8
$\frac{1}{2}bh$	$\frac{1}{2}(8 + 5)$
$2\ell + 2w$	$6 \times 8 \times 5$
ℓwh	$\frac{1}{2}(5)(6 + 8)$
$\frac{1}{2}h(b_1 + b_2)$	$2(6) + 2(8)$

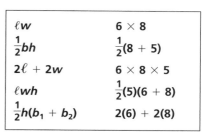

Did you know?
The ancient Mayan houses were so well-designed that many are still used today.

more ▶

Vocabulary 🔻 trapezoid

41

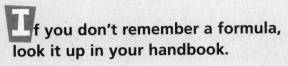

If you don't remember a formula, look it up in your handbook.

You're on the plane to your next destination but decide to do some calculations about the Mayan architecture while you are on the plane.

Temple of Kukulcan

Show how the parts of each problem are related by filling in the blanks.

6. You and Onatah want a replica of the Mayan Temple of Kukulcan in the exhibit. You remember from your visit there that the Temple is a truncated square pyramid. What area is covered by the Temple of Kukulcan? ◀MOC 366, 377

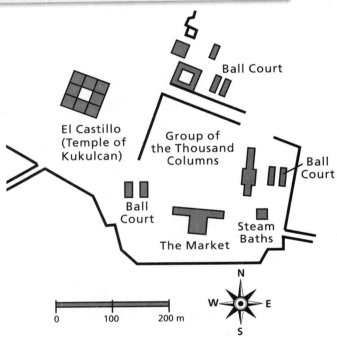

Ball Court

El Castillo (Temple of Kukulcan)

Group of the Thousand Columns

Ball Court

Ball Court

The Market

Steam Baths

   a. On the map, the temple is

   _____ long.

   b. Each centimeter on the map stands for

   _____ in real life.

   c. Area of the square ≈ _____ × _____

7. The Temple of Kukulcan is 79 feet high, including the top part. You use a photograph of you at the temple to estimate that the height of the top part of the temple is about 16 feet. The 4 stairways have a total of 364 steps. About how high is each step? (**HINT:** You may wish to draw a diagram.)

   a. Write and solve an equation for the number of steps on each stairway.

   b. Write and solve an equation for the height of each stairway.

   c. Write an expression to represent the height of each step. _____

42   Vocabulary ▼ truncated ▼ square pyramid ▼ height

8. Study the diagram. Each wall of the
Chichén-Itzá ball court has an area
of 7344 square feet. What is the area
of the part of the ball court that is
between the two walls? ◀MOC 366

The rectangular side-walls of the ball court
at Chichén-Itzá do not run the full length of
the court.

   a. Write the formula for area of a rectangle.

   _____

   b. Write and solve an equation to find the
length of a rectangular wall.

   c. Write an expression to represent the area
of the ball court between the walls.

   _____

9. In the exhibit, you want to help people understand
how much space people had in some ancient cities
compared to modern ones. Nearly 12,000 people
lived in Mayapán, which covered about $2\frac{1}{2}$ square
miles. How does the population density of
Mayapán compare to Mexico City, which has
2328 people per square kilometer? ◀MOC 537

Did you know?
The people from Chichén-Itzá moved
west and founded the city Mayapán
in the second half of the 13th century.

   a. Write an expression representing the population density of Mayapán in people
per square mile.

   _____

   b. Look up the number of kilometers in 1 mile. _____

   c. Write and solve an equation to find the number of square kilometers in
1 square mile.

   _____

   d. Write an expression to represent the difference between the population densities
of Mexico City and Mayapán.

   _____

Vocabulary ▾ formula

You can use what you know about relationships in a problem to make a plan.

Hidatsa Earthlodge

Knowing how the pieces of a house go together is not enough to build the house. You need a plan for putting the pieces together in a way that works. It's like that with math problems, too. You need to know how the pieces go together, but you should also have a plan for putting the pieces together to solve the problem.

You've arrived in the Dakotas where you plan to learn about Hidatsa architecture.

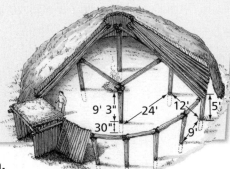

Circle the plan that you could use to solve the problem.

1. Study the diagram. The central posts in this replica of a Hidatsa earthlodge will be buried so that $2\frac{1}{2}$ feet of each post is below ground. To make this post, how much will be left after cutting the post from a log that is $14\frac{1}{2}$ feet long? ◀MOC 536

Plan A

- Write all measures in feet and inches.
- Add the underground length and the aboveground length to find the total length of the post.
- Subtract the length needed for the post from the length of the log.

Plan B

- Write all measurements in feet and inches.
- Subtract the underground length from the aboveground length to find the total length of the post.
- Add the total length needed for the post to the length of the log.

2. Use this diagram to find the length of the overhanging part of the 16-foot rafter. ◀MOC 359

Plan A

- Add 4.25 feet and 12 feet.
- Subtract the sum from 16 feet to find the length of the overhang.

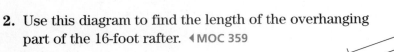
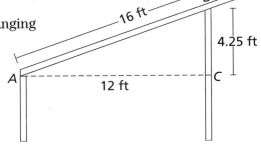

Plan B

THINK: The part of the rafter from A to B is the hypotenuse of right triangle ABC.

- Use the Pythagorean theorem to find the distance AB.
- Subtract AB from 16 feet to find the length of the overhang.

You want to learn about the longhouses that were built by the Iroquois.

12'

6'

110'

25'

3. To help estimate the cost of reconstructing the longhouse, you need to know its surface area. What is the surface area in square feet of all of the walls and flat roofs of the longhouse? Both flat roofs are the same size. ◂MOC 396

Plan A

- Use the formula for the area of a rectangle to find the area of the side.

    Area of side $= \ell w$

    $= 6(110)$

- Use the formula for the area of a rectangle to find the area of the flat roof section.

    Area of flat roof section $= \ell w$

    $= 25(110)$

- Add the areas to find the total surface area of the bottom part of the longhouse.

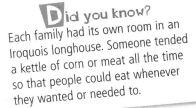

Did you know?
Each family had its own room in an Iroquois longhouse. Someone tended a kettle of corn or meat all the time so that people could eat whenever they wanted or needed to.

Plan B

- Use the formula for the area of a rectangle four times to find the area of the vertical surfaces.

    Area of vertical surfaces $= 6(110) + 6(110) + 6(25) + 6(25)$

- Use the formula for the area of a rectangle twice to find the area of the horizontal surfaces.

    Area of horizontal surfaces $= 12(25) + 12(25)$

- Add all the areas to find the total surface area of the bottom part of the longhouse.

more ▸

Vocabulary ▾ surface area

45

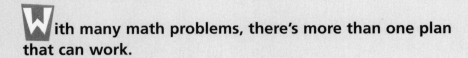

With many math problems, there's more than one plan that can work.

Now you're off to California to see the dwellings of the Yuroks.

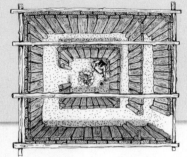 

Many Yurok family houses had two sets of plank walls with insulation space between them.

Circle the plan or plans that you could use to solve the problem.

4. Your reconstruction of the Yurok family house will be 24 feet by 21 feet and will have double-plank walls. If you use planks with an average width of 16 inches, about how many planks will you need for the four walls? ◀MOC 365 (HINT: Ignore doors and windows.)

Plan A

- To find the perimeter of the house, add 24 ft + 24 ft + 21 ft + 21 ft.
- Think of 16 inches as $1\frac{1}{3}$ feet.
- To find the number of planks for one set of walls, divide the perimeter $1\frac{1}{3}$.
- Multiply the number of planks by 2 to account for 2 sets of walls.

Plan B

- To find the perimeter of the house, use the formula: 2(24 ft) + 2(21 ft)
- To change feet to inches, multiply the perimeter by 12.
- To find the number of planks for one set of walls, divide the perimeter by 16.
- Multiply the number of planks by 2 to account for 2 sets of walls.

Complete the plan.

5. The living space of the Yurok family house will be a square 14 feet long. What percent of the floor area will be living space? ◀MOC 366, 444

Plan

- To find the _____ of the living space, multiply _____ by _____.

- To find the floor area of the whole house, _____ 24 by 21.

- To find the percent, set up and solve a proportion: $\dfrac{\boxed{}}{\text{total area}} = \dfrac{x}{100}$

46 Vocabulary ▼ perimeter

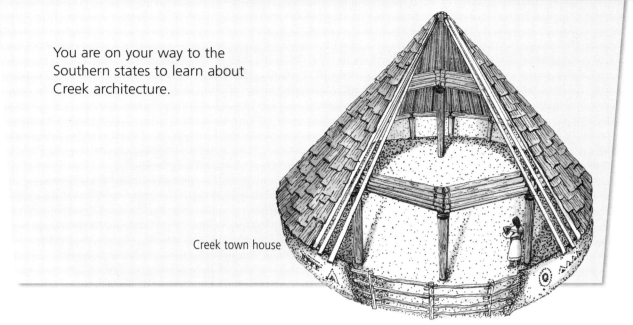

You are on your way to the Southern states to learn about Creek architecture.

Creek town house

6. What is the length of the sloping roof rafter in this plan for a replica of Creek town house? ◂MOC 358–359

Plan

THINK: The roof rafter, c, is the _____ of a right triangle.

- Fill in what you know in the

  _____ Theorem:

  $15^2 +$ _____ $= c^2$

- Solve the equation for c.

- The answer will be in _____.

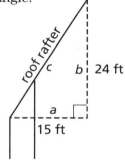

Complete both plans for solving problem 7.

7. You have figured out that the area of the roof of the Creek town house is 403 square yards. It costs $3.00 per square foot for bark shingles for the roof. How much will it cost to cover the entire roof? ◂MOC 153

Plan A

- To change the area from square yards to square feet, multiply _____ by _____.

- Multiply the area in square feet by _____.

Plan B

- To change the cost per square foot to the cost per square yard,

  _____ $3.00 per square foot by _____.

- Multiply the cost per square yard by _____.

more ▸

47

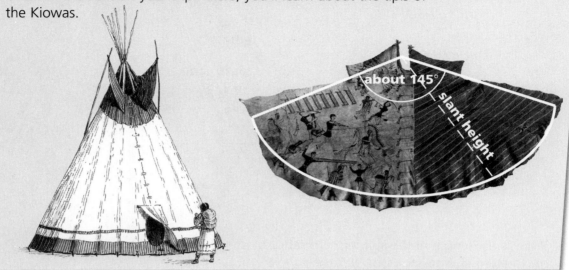

Having a plan that works is a key to problem solving.

Oklahoma is next on your trip. There, you'll learn about the tipis of the Kiowas.

Complete the plan that you could use to solve the problem. If both plans can work, complete them both.

8. Not counting the flaps, about how much animal hide was used for a tipi with a slant height of 12 feet? ◄MOC 340, 374, 375

   THINK: The flattened-out tipi skin looks like a sector of a _____.

   Plan A

   • To find what fraction of a circle the sector represents, divide 145 by _____.

   • Fill in what you know in the formula for the area of a circle:

   $A = \pi r^2$

   = _____

   • To find the area of the sector, _____.

   Plan B

   • Fill in what you know in the formula for the area of a circle:

   $A = \pi r^2$

   = _____

   • Set up and solve a proportion:

   $$\dfrac{\text{Area of sector} \rightarrow \boxed{}}{\text{Area of circle} \rightarrow \boxed{}} = \dfrac{\boxed{}}{\boxed{}}$$

Vocabulary ▼ slant height ▼ sector

This is quite a trip you are on. Now you are
in Peru to learn about Incan architecture.

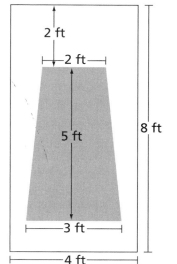

**Complete the plan that you could use to solve the
problem. If both plans can work, complete them both.**

9. The diagram shows the dimensions of your reconstruction
   of this Inca doorway. What is the area covered by the
   smooth stones around the opening? ◀MOC 366, 368

   THINK: The shape of the opening is a _____.

   Plan A

   • Ignore the opening and find the area of the whole rectangle:

     $A = \ell w$

     = _____

   • To find the area of the opening, use the formula for the
     area of a trapezoid:

     $A = \frac{1}{2}h(b_1 + b_2)$

     = _____

   • Find the area covered by the smooth stones by

     _____.

   Plan B

   • To find the area above the opening (▨), use the
     formula for area of a rectangle:

     $A = \ell w$

     = _____

   • To find the area of the stones below the opening (▥),
     use the formula for area of a rectangle:

     $A = \ell w$

     = _____

   • To find the area of the stones on both sides of the
     opening (▢), use the formula for area of a trapezoid:

     $A(\text{one side}) = \frac{1}{2}h(b_1 + b_2)$

     $A(\text{both sides}) =$ _____

   • Find the area covered by smooth stones by _____.

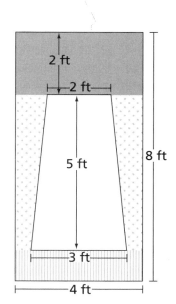

more ▶

49

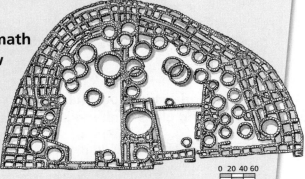

When you make a plan to solve a math problem, think about what you know and what you are trying to find out.

You've decided to end your tour with a trip to Chaco Canyon to learn about the ancient Anasazi culture by looking at Pueblo Bonito and Casa Rinconada.

Pueblo Bonito

0 20 40 60
Scale in Feet

Write a plan for solving each problem.

10. Study the diagram. What is a reasonable estimate of the area covered by Pueblo Bonito?

Did you know?
Pueblo Bonito means *pretty village* in Spanish.

Plan

_____

_____

_____

11. If a circular kiva with a radius of 8 feet is in a square enclosure 16 feet on a side, what percent of the area of the square is taken up by the kiva? ◀ MOC 366, 375, 444

Plan

The ruins at Chaco Canyon have many round rooms called kivas.

_____

_____

_____

12. One researcher estimates that it took 45,000 kilograms of stone, 15,000 kilograms of clay, and 4,100 liters of water to construct a single room in Pueblo Bonito. How many tons of material is that? (**HINT:** 1 liter of water has a mass of 1 kilogram.) ◀ MOC 537

Plan

_____

_____

_____

_____

50

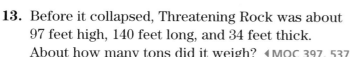

13. Before it collapsed, Threatening Rock was about 97 feet high, 140 feet long, and 34 feet thick. About how many tons did it weigh?   ◂MOC 397, 537

Plan

_____

_____

_____

_____

_____

Before 1941, Threatening Rock, a sandstone monolith, weighed about 130 pounds per cubic foot.

14. Casa Rinconada is 63 feet in diameter and about 15 feet deep. A room in Pueblo Bonito might be 14 feet long, 9 feet wide, and $7\frac{1}{2}$ feet high. About how many of these rooms could fit into Casa Rinconada?   ◂MOC 397, 413

Plan

_____

_____

_____

_____

_____

_____

_____

_____

_____

In 1941 Threatening Rock fell and crushed part of Pueblo Bonito.

Casa Rinconada in Chaco Canyon

You are amazed at the variety of Native American architecture. You can hardly wait to begin building the village with Onatah Wanyandie.

Vocabulary ▪ cubic foot (ft³)

51

Fill in the circle with the letter of the correct answer.

1. Which relationship will best help you find the measure of angle *S*?

   A The measures of complementary angles have a sum of 90°.

   B The measures of supplementary angles have a sum of 180°.

   C The measures of the angles of a triangle have a sum of 180°.

   D The base angles of an isosceles triangle are congruent.

2. The diagram shows a brick border of a garden. To find the approximate length of each brick, divide the _____ of the circle by the number of bricks.

   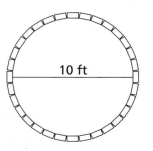

   A area

   B circumference

   C diameter

   D radius

3. A city of 38,000 people is in the shape of a rectangle 5 kilometers long and 3 kilometers wide. Which expression tells you the number of people per square kilometer in the city?

   A $38,000 \times 5 \times 3$

   B $\frac{5}{3 \times 38,000}$

   C $\frac{38,000}{5 \times 3}$

   D none of these

4. You want to find how much paint you need to paint all six sides of a large rectangular box. Which formula will help you most?

   A $A = \pi r^2$

   B $A = \frac{1}{2}bh$

   C $V = \ell wh$

   D $A = \ell w$

5. Tyler's computer has taken 1 minute 20 seconds to download 40% of a file. If the computer continues at that rate, which proportion could Tyler use to find the number of seconds needed for the entire download?

   A $\frac{40}{100} = \frac{80}{x}$

   B $\frac{120}{40} = \frac{x}{100}$

   C $\frac{x}{80} = \frac{40}{100}$

   D none of these

Write a plan that you could use to solve the problem.

6. A 5-inch by 7-inch photo is placed in an 8-inch by 10-inch frame. What is the area inside the frame that is not covered by the photo? (HINT: Complete the diagram to help you write your plan.)

Plan

_____

_____

_____

_____

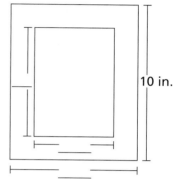

10 in.

Write a proportion or other equation that you could solve to answer the question.

7. A 5 foot by 3 foot rectangular banner is all red except for a green triangle that is 2 feet high and has a base of 2 feet. What percent of the banner is red? (HINT: Complete the diagram to help you write your equation.)

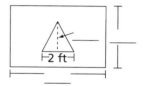

2 ft

_____

Write a problem that could be solved using this equation.

8. $c = \sqrt{4.5^2 + 7^2}$

_____

_____

_____

Write a problem that could be solved using this plan.

9. • Find the product of 3.14 and 6^2.

• Multiply that product by \$3.50.

_____

_____

_____

4

RUSH FOR GOLD

Carrying Out the Plan

Found 30 ounces of gold. Forward 3 spaces.

Your ship sank. Back 2 spaces.

You've got fool's gold. Back 1 space.

In what year was gold found at Sutter's Mill?

3

5

Stream is panned out. Miss 1 turn.

54

In this chapter, you'll learn about one of the most exciting times in the history of the United States, the California Gold Rush. Be prepared for anything. You'll get practice preparing to solve problems, and you'll also be carefully carrying out those plans. You will use the second and third steps of the four-step problem-solving method: **Plan** and **Try**.

After gold was discovered in California, shipping companies helped spread gold fever with ads like this one.

▸ There were few women and children in the mining camps, but those who came worked hard, either mining or finding ways to support the miners. Luzena Wilson, for example, set up a sort of open-air restaurant near Sacramento in 1849 and later was a writer, banker, and innkeeper.

▾ There were many rumors about the amount of gold in California. People in the east heard about rivers that were paved in gold. They heard that all you had to do was go out for a walk and you would find gold nuggets to pick up all over the place.

Miner's Adaptation of *Oh! Susanna*

I soon shall be in San Francisco,
And then I'll look around,
And when I see the gold lumps there,
I'll pick them off the ground.

Oh, Californi-o,
That's the land for me!
I'm going to Sacramento,
With my washboard on my knee.

▴ Stephen Foster wrote *Oh! Susanna* in 1846. This song was very popular with miners heading for the gold fields of California. They made up many of their own lyrics to Foster's tune.

55

■nce you have a plan, it's important to carefully carry out your plan.

You've decided to enter the *Rush for Gold* tournament and you know you're going to need to brush up on your knowledge of the California Gold Rush. You decide to begin by looking at a time line.

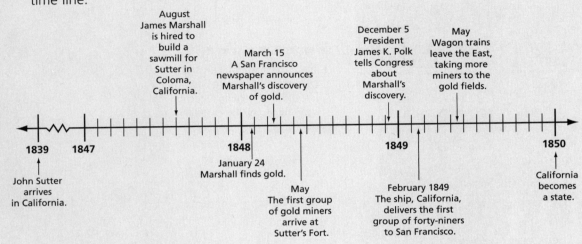

Read each problem and the plan for solving it. Circle the solution that correctly carries out that plan. Then complete the answer to the problem.

1. News did not travel as fast in the 1800s as it does today. Look at the period of time that starts with the day Marshall discovered gold and ends on the day President Polk announced it to Congress. How many days were in that period? (HINT: 1848 was a leap year.) ◀MOC 128, 536

Plan • Find the number of days in January before the day Marshall made his discovery.

• Find the number of days in December after the day Polk made his announcement.

• Subtract the sum of the results of the first two steps from the number of days in a leap year.

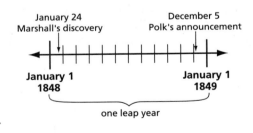

Try Circle the solution that correctly carries out the plan.

A. $366 - 23 + 26$

B. $366 - (26 - 23)$

C. $366 - (23 + 26)$

D. $26 - (366 - 23)$

Answer It was _____ days from the day gold was discovered through the day the president told Congress.

56   Vocabulary ▼ time line ▼ leap year

2. Of the approximately 85,000 people who came to California to look for gold in 1849, about 23,000 were *not* U. S. citizens. About what percent were U. S. citizens? ◀MOC 444, 126

Plan • Find the number of the people who were U. S. citizens.

• Find what percent that number is of 85,000.

Try Circle the solution that correctly carries out the plan.

A. $85,000 - 23,000 = 62,000$

$$\frac{62,000}{85,000} = \frac{62}{85}$$

$$\approx 0.73$$

$$0.73 = 73\%$$

B. $85,000 + 23,000 = 108,000$

$$\frac{62,000}{108,000} = \frac{62}{108}$$

$$\approx 0.57$$

$$0.57 = 57\%$$

C. $85,000 + 23,000 = 108,000$

$$\frac{23,000}{85,000} = \frac{23}{85}$$

$$\approx 0.27$$

$$0.27 = 27\%$$

Answer About _____% of the forty-niners were U. S. citizens.

---

3. The time line shows that the miners' wagon trains to California began in May of 1849. You are curious to find out how many women went on these journeys. You learn that a count was made at Fort Kearney. By May 21, 1849, about twenty-eight hundred wagons, carrying an average of 4.5 people per wagon, had passed through Fort Kearney. Only about 80 of those people were women. What was the approximate ratio of women to men? ◀MOC 424, 158–159

Plan • Find the approximate number of people in all of the wagons.

• Find the number of those people who were men.

• Write the ratio of women to men in simplest form.

Try Circle the solution that correctly carries out the plan.

A. $2800 \div 4.5 \approx 622$

$622 - 80 = 542$

$$\frac{80}{542} = \frac{40}{271}$$

B. $2800 \times 4.5 = 12,600$

$12,600 - 80 = 12,520$

$$\frac{12,520}{80} = \frac{313}{2}$$

C. $2800 \times 4.5 = 12,600$

$12,600 - 80 = 12,520$

$$\frac{80}{12,520} = \frac{2}{313}$$

Answer The ratio of women to men was about _____.

There is often more than one plan you can use to solve a problem.

There were three ways that people from the East could get to California by ship. They could travel around Cape Horn; take a shortcut through the Strait of Magellan; or sail to Panama, cross the Isthmus of Panama on foot, then sail on to San Francisco. There were also several overland routes. The map here shows the Oregon Trail with the California cutoff.

Read each problem and the plan for solving it. Carry out that plan. Then complete the answer to the problem.

1. The *Sea Eagle* took 36 days to make the 150-mile journey through the Strait of Magellan. If the boat was moving forward 24 hours a day, what was its average speed through the Strait in miles per hour? ◄MOC 154, 179

Plan • To find the number of hours in 36 days, multiply 36 by 24.

• Divide the distance traveled by the number of hours.

Try

Answer The *Sea Eagle's* average speed was about _____ miles per hour.

---

2. The San Francisco Custom House records for 1849 show that 15,597 immigrants arrived in San Francisco via Cape Horn and 6489 took the shortcut across the Isthmus of Panama. What percent of these seafaring newcomers took the shortcut? ◄MOC 444

Plan • To find the total number of immigrants, find the sum of 15,597 and 6489.

• To find the percent of newcomers who took the shortcut, set up and solve a proportion: $\frac{x}{100} = \frac{6489}{sum}$

Try

Answer About _____% of the immigrants arriving by sea took the shortcut across the Isthmus of Panama.

Vocabulary ▼ proportion

3. Look back at problem 1. You used a plan that called for multiplying and then dividing. Write an expression to show how you can you solve the problem by dividing twice.

_____

4. Look back at problem 2. You solved the problem by writing a proportion. Show how you can you solve the problem with a different kind of equation.

_____

Since the land trip was so much shorter than any of the sea routes, you wonder why anyone would choose to travel by sea. Then you learn that traveling by sea was quite comfortable compared to traveling by land where food ran low, water was scarce, and herds of buffalo scared the horses and mules that pulled the wagons.

5. The sea route around Cape Horn was about 15,000 miles from New York to San Francisco. About how many times as long as the overland route was the sea route? (**HINT:** It was about 1000 miles from New York to Independence by land.) ◂MOC 179–181, 377

Plan • Measure the overland route on the map.

• Use the scale on the map to find the length of the overland route in miles.

• Divide the length of the sea route by the length of the overland route.

• Round the answer to the nearest whole number.

Try

Answer The sea route was about _____ times as long as the overland route.

Vocabulary ▾ scale on the map

Choosing the Plan and Solving the Problem

Be sure you carry out each step of the plan.

You learn that, to pan for gold, a miner stood in a river and scooped up sand and water and swirled it in the pan. The sand or dirt swirled to the edges of the pan. What was left in the bottom of the pan was gold. This worked because gold is more dense than sand or dirt.

Follow the steps to solve the problem.

1. Three miners gathered 45 ounces of gold one day, 38 ounces the next day, and 51 ounces the following day. What was the value of that gold? ◀MOC 101, 154

Plan Circle the plan that works.

Plan A
- To find the total number of ounces gathered, add 45, 38, and 51.
- To find the value, multiply the sum by 16.
- The answer will be in dollars.

Plan B
- To find the total number of ounces gathered, add 45, 38, and 51.
- To find the value, divide the sum by 16.
- The answer will be in dollars.

Try Carry out the plan you circled. Write the answer as a complete sentence.

2. A 14-year-old boy spent 54 days panning for gold and collected gold worth $3,467.00. If he collected about the same number of ounces every day, about how much gold did he collect per day? ◀MOC 179–181

Plan Circle the plan that works.

Plan A
- To find the mean number of dollars per day, divide 3467 by 54.
- To find the mean number of ounces per day, multiply the quotient by 16.
- The answer will be in ounces.

Plan B
- To find the total number of ounces, divide 3467 by 16.
- To find the mean number of ounces per day, divide the quotient by 54.
- The answer will be in ounces.

Try Carry out the plan you circled. Write the answer as a complete sentence.

60

Gold panning was slow. It took about 20 minutes to get the gold particles out of a pan. A sluice was a series of boxes through which water could move faster. Gold particles were caught by the bars in the boxes as the water moved through.

3. The faster the water moves, the larger the pebble that it can move. The diameter of the moved pebble is proportional to the square of the speed of the water. If a 2-inch pebble can be rolled along by water moving at 9 feet per second, how fast would water need to move to carry along a pebble 8 inches in diameter? ◀ MOC 434

Circle the plan that works.

Plan A

- Set up a proportion
  $$\frac{\text{small size}}{\text{large size}} = \frac{(\text{slow speed})^2}{(\text{fast speed})^2}$$
- Substitute the known values and solve
  $$\frac{2}{8} = \frac{9^2}{x^2}$$
- The result is in feet per second.

Plan B

- Set up a proportion
  $$\frac{\text{small size}}{\text{large size}} = \frac{\text{slow speed}}{\text{fast speed}}$$
- Substitute the known values and solve
  $$\frac{2}{8} = \frac{9}{x}$$
- The result is in feet per second.

Carry out the plan you circled. Write the answer as a complete sentence.

4. Study the diagram of a sluice. Suppose the length of each trough was 12 feet and there was 16 inches of overlap where each pair of troughs met. What would be the length of a 5-trough sluice? ◀ MOC 163, 132

16 in.

12 ft

Circle the plan that works.

Plan A

- To find the length of 5 separate 12-foot troughs, multiply 5 by 12.
- **THINK:** 16 inches = $1\frac{1}{3}$ feet. To find the length of the overlaps, multiply 4 by $1\frac{1}{3}$.
- Subtract to find the overall length in feet.

Plan B

- To find the length of 5 separate 12-foot troughs, multiply 5 by 12.
- **THINK:** 16 inches = $1\frac{1}{3}$ feet. To find the length of the overlaps, multiply 5 by $1\frac{1}{3}$.
- Subtract to find the overall length in feet.

Carry out the plan you circled. Write the answer as a complete sentence.

Vocabulary ▪ feet per second

61

Menu for Ward House			
Baked trout	$1.50	Sweet potatoes	$0.50
Roast beef	$1.00	Irish potatoes	$0.50
Roast lamb	$1.00	Cabbage	$0.50
Roast pork	$1.25	**Desserts:**	
Corned beef	$1.25	Bread pudding	$0.75
Ham	$1.00	Mince pie	$0.75
Lamb	$1.25	Cheese	$0.50
Fresh egg	$1.00	Prunes	$0.75

As you carry out your plan, check that the result in each step is reasonable.

Some of the menu items from a San Francisco hotel in 1849.

Refer to the menu to make plans and solve these problems.

1. If you bought a meat item for $1.00, a potato item for 50¢, a vegetable for 50¢, and a dessert for 75¢, you could have a meal for $2.75. How many different meals like this are possible? ◄MOC 460, 464

Plan Fill in the blanks.

- Find the number of each item that has the price listed:

    Meat _____   Potato _____

    Vegetable _____   Dessert _____

- Make an organized list or tree diagram.

- Count the possible meals.

Try Carry out your plan. Write the answer as a complete sentence.

_____

2. How could you solve problem 1 by multiplying instead of by making a list or diagram?

_____

3. A miner ordered baked trout, sweet potatoes, and mince pie. He paid with $\frac{1}{4}$ ounce of gold. If his change was $3.00, what was the value of his gold in dollars per ounce? ◄MOC 241

Plan Fill in the blanks

- Write an equation in words: Amount paid − _____ = change received

- Add to find the cost of the meal: _____ + _____ + _____

- Let x represent the value of 1 ounce of gold.

- Substitute known values and solve: $\frac{1}{4}x$ − _____ = _____

Try Carry out the plan. Write the answer as a complete sentence.

_____

62   Vocabulary ▼ tree diagram

Hard rock miners had to find a way to separate the gold in the rock from everything else. They did this by crushing the rock. An arrastra was one tool they used.

Complete the plans and solve the problems.

4. An arrastra was powered by a mule walking in a circle at the rate of about 8 revolutions per minute. It took about $3\frac{1}{2}$ hours to crush one load of ore. About how many times did the mule go around the circle in that time? ◂MOC 163, 536

Plan Fill in the blanks

- To find the number of _____ in _____ hours, multiply $3\frac{1}{2}$ by _____.

- To find the number of revolutions, multiply _____ by _____.

Try Carry out your plan. Write the answer as a complete sentence.

_____

5. At the Kennedy mine, each mining wheel was 68 feet in diameter and had 176 buckets. If the buckets were equally spaced around the rim, about how far would it be along the rim from the center of one bucket to the center of the next? ◂MOC 372

Plan Fill in the blanks.

- To find the distance around the rim, use

  the formula for _____.

- To find the distance in feet from bucket-center to bucket-center, _____

  the circumference by _____.

Try Carry out the plan. Write the answer as a complete sentence.

_____

more ▸

Sometimes your plan might involve proportions, formulas, and other equations.

You decide you should learn something about the properties of gold before you enter the *Rush for Gold* tournament. You find a table that tells you the density of gold and other substances. Density can be measured in grams per cubic centimeter.

Density of Gold and Other Substances

Substance	Density $\left(\frac{g}{cm^3}\right)$
gold	19.3
pyrite	5.0
silver	10.49
aluminum	2.708
iron	7.87
lead	11.34

Did you know?
Pyrite is often called fool's gold because it looks so much like gold. Many miners thought they had struck it rich, only to find out that they had found fool's gold.

Read the problem. Complete and carry out the plan. Then write the answer as a complete sentence.

6. The mass of a gold brick is 12.5 kilograms. What would be the mass of a same-size brick made of fool's gold? ◄MOC 434

Plan Fill in the blanks

- Let x represent the mass of the pyrite brick.

- Set up a proportion: $\dfrac{\text{mass of 1 cm}^3 \text{ of gold}}{\text{mass of 1 cm}^3 \text{ of pyrite}} = \dfrac{\text{mass of _____ brick}}{\text{mass of _____ brick}}$

- Substitute the known values: $\dfrac{\Box}{\Box} = \dfrac{\Box}{\Box}$

- Solve for _____.

Try Carry out the plan. Write the answer as a complete sentence.

7. Gold is *malleable*—it can be pounded into a very thin sheet. One ounce of gold can be hammered into a sheet that covers 100 square feet. What is the thickness of such a sheet? ◂MOC 397, 241

Plan Fill in the blanks.

THINK: The volume of an ounce of gold is _____ cubic inches.

- Write an equation in words: volume of sheet = area of sheet × _____.

- To change 100 square feet to square inches, multiply 100 by _____.

- Let x represent _____. Substitute the known values into your equation.

_____

- Solve for _____.

Try Carry out the plan. Write the answer as a complete sentence.

_____

---

8. Gold is *ductile*—it can be stretched. One ounce of gold can form a 50-mile long wire. What would be the radius of such a wire? ◂MOC 413, 536, 241

$r = ?$

$h = 50$ mi

Plan Fill in the blanks.

THINK: The gold wire weighs 1 ounce, so its volume is _____ cubic inches.

- To change 50 miles to feet, multiply 50 by _____.

- To change to inches, multiply that product by _____.

- Use the formula for the volume of a _____.

$V = \pi r^2 h$

_____ $\approx (3.14)r^2($_____$)$

- Solve for _____.

Try Carry out the plan. Write the answer as a complete sentence.

_____

Sometimes your plan won't match your friend's plan.

Many of the miners took their gold to the United States branch mint in San Francisco. In 1854, the first year of operation, the mint produced 4 million dollars worth of gold coins. By 1856, the mint was producing nearly $24 million worth of gold coins a year.

$20 Double Eagle

$10 Eagle

$5 Half Eagle

$3 Gold Piece

$2.50 Quarter Eagle

Study the coins above. Then follow the directions.

1. A museum display contains 4 gold coins like the ones above.
   What coins are in the display if their total face value is $18.50?

Plan _____

_____

_____

Try Show your work. Write your answer as a complete sentence.

_____

2. Refer to the coins at the top of the page. Find the number of different combinations
   of coins like these with a face value of $22.00. ◄MOC 460

Plan _____

_____

Try Show your work. Write your answer as a complete sentence.

_____

You discover that people use special units to measure gold. For example, *carats* are used to measure the purity of gold, and *troy ounces* and *troy pounds* are used to measure the weight of gold.

Measures of Gold Purity		
24 carats	=	$\frac{24}{24}$ gold
18 carats	=	$\frac{18}{24}$ gold
14 carats	=	$\frac{14}{24}$ gold

Some Gold Conversions
1 troy ounce = 1.1 customary ounces
1 customary ounce = 0.91 troy ounces
troy pound = 12 troy ounces
1 troy pound = 0.37 kilograms

3. Jewelry is never made with 24-carat gold because it would be too soft. A 14-carat bracelet contains gold mixed with 1.2 customary ounces of other metal. How many troy ounces of gold are in the bracelet?

Plan _____

_____

_____

_____

Try Show your work. Write your answer as a complete sentence.

_____

more ▶

Sometimes your plan might involve finding information from a graph.

Complete and carry out each plan.

4. Study the graph. During which period did gold production show a greater percent increase, from 1849 to 1850 or from 1850 to 1851? ◀MOC 298, 447

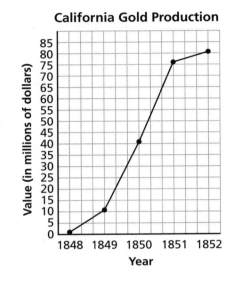

California Gold Production

Plan _____

_____

_____

_____

_____

Try Show your work. Write your answer as a complete sentence.

_____

5. In 1857, a company spent $177,000 on mining and found $252,000 worth of gold. How much was the profit as a percent of the amount they invested? ◀MOC 444

Plan _____

_____

_____

Try Show your work. Write your answer as a complete sentence.

_____

68

Gold Mined Worldwide through 1986:
121,000 tons

6. Refer to the smudged graph. About how many tons of gold were owned by private individuals in 1986? ◀MOC 296

29%
Gold bars held
by national banks

15%
Gold used
and can't be
recovered

Gold owned
by private individuals
(jewelry, coins, etc.)

Plan _____

_____

_____

_____

_____

Try Show your work. Write your answer as a complete sentence.

_____

---

7. An official U. S. gold brick weighs about 28 pounds. The density of gold is 0.7 pounds per cubic inch. Based on this information and the photo, which of these could be the dimensions of the base of an official U. S. gold brick? ◀MOC 397

A. 14 inches by $7\frac{1}{4}$ inches by $3\frac{1}{2}$ inches

B. 7 inches by $3\frac{5}{8}$ inches by $1\frac{3}{4}$ inches

C. 5 inches by $4\frac{1}{2}$ inches by 2 inches?

Plan _____

_____

Try Show your work. Write your answer as a complete sentence.

_____

You've really learned a lot about gold and the California gold rush, and you've decided you are ready to play in the *Rush for Gold* tournament. Good luck!

Fill in the circle with the letter of the correct answer.

1. Which solution is a correct way to find what percent 27 is of 135?

   (A) $\frac{27}{100} = \frac{x}{135}$

   $100x = 27 \times 135$

   $100x = 3{,}645$

   $x = 36.45$

   (B) $\frac{27}{135} = \frac{x}{100}$

   $27x = 135 \times 100$

   $27x = 13{,}500$

   $x \approx 55.6$

   (C) $\frac{x}{100} = \frac{27}{135}$

   $135x = 27 \times 100$

   $135x = 2{,}700$

   $x = 20$

2. The formula for the volume of a cylinder is $V = \pi r^2 h$. Which expression represents the volume in cubic feet of a cylindrical tube that is 5 feet long and has a diameter of 6 inches?

   (A) $3.14 \times \left(\frac{1}{2}\right)^2 \times 5$

   (B) $3.14 \times \left(\frac{1}{4}\right)^2 \times 5$

   (C) $3.14 \times 6^2 \times 5$

   (D) $3.14 \times 3^2 \times 5$

3. A baby was born on March 3, 2001. Which expression tells how many days old the baby was on May 15, 2003?

   (A) $(2003 - 2001) + (28 + 30 + 15)$

   (B) $3(365) - (28 + 30 + 15)$

   (C) $2(365) + (28 + 30 + 15)$

   (D) $2(365) - (28 + 30 + 15)$

**For exercises 4–5, write your plan in the box. Then carry out the plan.
Fill in the circle with the letter of the correct answer.**

4. How much will it cost to buy 3 CDs priced at $13.50 each and 2 DVDs priced at $19 each?

   (A) $60.50

   (B) $41.50

   (C) $32.50

   (D) $78.50

5. What is the weight of a 3-centimeter cube if it is made of a material with a density of 4 grams per cubic centimeter?

   (A) 12 grams

   (B) 36 g grams

   (C) 108 grams

   (D) 12 kilograms

For exercise 6, fill in the circle with the letter of the correct answer. Explain why you made your choice.

6. In an election, Trish received 340 votes. The other 45% of votes were for Val. Which equation could you solve to find the number of students who voted in the election?

A $(0.45)(340) = x$ _____

B $0.45x = 340$ _____

C $0.55x = 340$ _____

D $100 - 0.55 = x - 0.45$ _____

Write a plan and solve.

7. You bike from 10:45 A.M. to 1:15 P.M. and travel a distance of 45 miles. What is your average speed?

_____

_____

_____

_____

Solve this problem in two different ways.

8. Part of the scenery for a school play is shown in the diagram. What is the area of the shaded section?

My first plan:

_____

_____

_____

Answer _____

My second plan:

_____

_____

_____

Answer _____

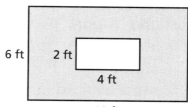

6 ft   2 ft   4 ft   10 ft

Above the World

Looking Back

Expedition to Top of the World Needs Reporter

An expedition to Mount Everest, the highest mountain in the world, is looking for a student reporter. The selected applicant will hike with the group to Everest Base Camp and report over the Internet about the journey to the summit. Through these reports, students in schools all over the country will be able to learn about Everest and track the progress of the climb.

If you are interested in this opportunity, send your application to this newspaper. Include a letter about why you want the job.

In this chapter, you will travel to the highest mountain in the world. You'll find out about Mount Everest and *look back* at the many attempts over the years to reach its summit. You'll also learn how to *look back* at a math problem after you've solved it. You won't always be able to know whether you've solved a problem correctly. However, you should often catch errors in reasoning or computation in time to fix them. You will get lots of practice using the fourth step in the four-step problem-solving method: **Look Back.**

▼ There is a debate about who was the first person to reach the top of Mount Everest. Most say Sir Edmund Hillary and Tenzing Norgay were the first to reach the top, in 1953. However, George Mallory and Andrew Irvine may have reached the top in 1924. Nobody knows for sure, because they never returned. Mallory's body, preserved by the cold, was found in 1999.

▲ The first aerial photograph of Mount Everest was taken from a biplane in 1933.

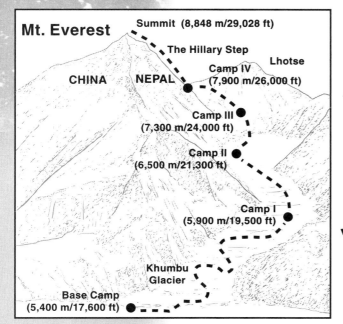

Mt. Everest

Summit (8,848 m/29,028 ft)

The Hillary Step

Lhotse

Camp IV
(7,900 m/26,000 ft)

CHINA   NEPAL

Camp III
(7,300 m/24,000 ft)

Camp II
(6,500 m/21,300 ft)

Camp I
(5,900 m/19,500 ft)

Khumbu
Glacier

Base Camp
(5,400 m/17,600 ft)

◀ Before getting to the summit of Mount Everest, the climbers first trek for about 12 days from Kathmandu to Everest Base Camp. Then, they climb in careful stages to Camps I, II, III, and IV, moving up and down among the camps until their bodies can function in the low-oxygen environment they will encounter on the way to the summit. Many climbing groups plan for the round trip from Base Camp and back to Base Camp to take about 40 days.

Always look back to make sure you answered the question.

You applied for the Mount Everest reporter job and got it! Now you want to learn about Mount Everest and some of the other tall mountains in the world. You find this bar graph that shows the height of the tallest mountain on each of the seven continents.

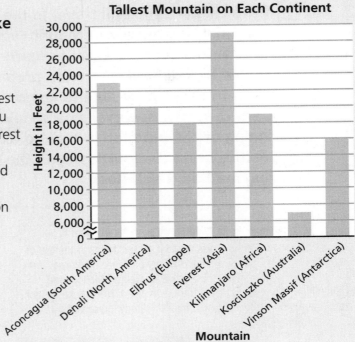

Tallest Mountain on Each Continent

Circle the choice that answers the question asked.

1. About how many feet higher is Mount Everest than the next highest mountain on the graph? ◄MOC 292

   A. Mount Everest is about 25% higher than the next highest mountain on the graph.

   B. The second highest mountain on the graph is 22,840 feet high.

   C. Mount Everest is about 6000 feet higher than the next highest mountain on the graph.

2. On which continent does the highest peak have an elevation of less than 2 miles? ◄MOC 292

   A. Mount Kosciuszko has an elevation of less than 2 miles.

   B. The highest peak in Australia is under 2 miles high.

   C. The elevation of Mount Kosciuszko is 7310 feet, which is less than 10,560 feet.

Did you find that you could answer each question just by looking for an answer that seemed to match the question? When solving a math problem, it's important to ▶**Look Back** at your answer to see whether it matches the question. For example, if a problem asks for a measurement, be sure your answer is a measurement; if a problem asks for a name, be sure your answer is a name.

You learn more about Everest when you find a timeline.

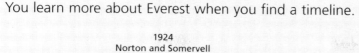

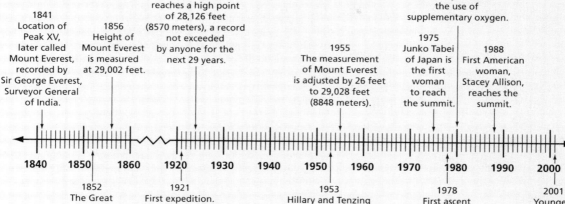

For questions 3–6, choose the letter of the correct answer from this box.

_____ **3.** How long after the first expedition was the summit of Mount Everest reached? ◀ MOC 128

_____ **4.** In what year was the first ascent to an altitude higher than 28,126 feet? ◀ MOC 099

_____ **5.** By what percent was the measurement of Mount Everest adjusted in 1955? ◀ MOC 444

_____ **6.** What was the first measured height of Mount Everest in kilometers? ◀ MOC 537

A.	**29,002 feet**
B.	**1921 to 1953**
C.	**8.8 kilometers**
D.	**26 feet**
E.	**1953**
F.	**0.09%**
G.	**32 years**

7. How did you choose the correct answers without calculating?

_____

_____

_____

_____

_____

Always look back to be sure you've used the correct unit in your answer.

When you give your answer to a math problem, labels are very important. For example, one hour is very different from one minute, or one second, or one day.

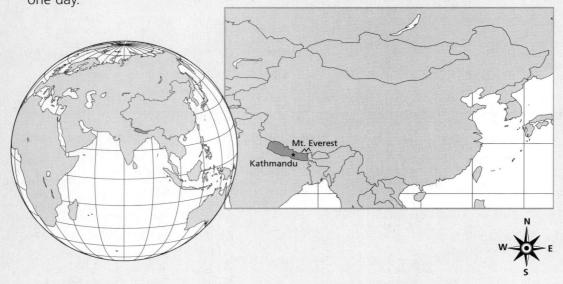

Use units listed in the box to complete the answers. You may use some units more than once and some not at all.

1. Your plane takes off from Los Angeles at 10:45 P.M. on March 24 and lands in Kathmandu on March 26 at 12:45 P.M. Kathmandu is 23 hours ahead of Pacific Standard Time. How long does the flight take? ◀MOC 536

   Answer 25 _____

2. Mount Everest is at 86°56' East Longitude, 27°59' North Latitude. Kathmandu is at 85°19' East Longitude, 27°42' North Latitude. How far east of Kathmandu is Mount Everest? ◀MOC 583–584, 128

   Answer 1 _____ 37 _____

3. Sir Edmund Hillary's expedition to Mount Everest carried 473 packages. If each package weighed between 25 and 35 pounds, what was the maximum possible weight of the packages? ◀MOC 154

   Answer 16,555 _____

degree
degrees Celsius
degrees Fahrenheit
feet
feet per hour
hours
miles
minutes
%
pounds
square yards
years

Vocabulary ▼ degrees Celsius (°C) ▼ degrees Fahrenheit (°F) ▼ Pacific Standard Time
▼ degrees (°) and minutes (') of longitude ▼ degrees (°) and minutes (') of latitude

76

  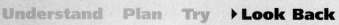
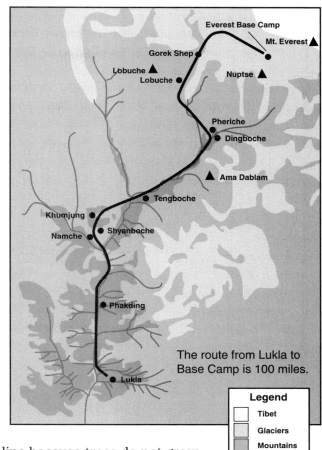

4. When you reach Dingboche, you are about $\frac{3}{5}$ of the way along the route from Lukla to Base Camp. About how far is it from Dingboche to Base Camp? ◂MOC 161

   Answer About 40 _____

5. Everest Base Camp is about the area of 4 football fields. How large is that? ◂MOC 153, 366, 536

   Answer
   About 24,000 _____

6. Because Earth's crust continues to shift, Mount Everest is getting taller at a rate of $\frac{1}{6}$ inch per year. At that rate, how long will it take to grow 5 feet? ◂MOC 189, 536

   Answer 360 _____

The route from Lukla to Base Camp is 100 miles.

Legend
Tibet
Glaciers
Mountains
River Valley

7. The elevation of 11,000 feet is called the tree line because trees do not grow above that altitude. About how far above the tree line is Base Camp? (**HINT:** Look back at page 73.) ◂MOC 126, 536

   Answer About 1.1 _____

8. You learn that the fastest ascent to the summit from Base Camp was 16 hours and 45 minutes. What was the average climbing rate for that ascent? ◂MOC 274, 536

   Answer 1733 _____

Base Camp on Mount Everest

77

You can use your number sense to tell when an answer is too large or too small to be correct.

Sherpas live in the mountainous area of Nepal. They are strong climbers in the thin air because they live at high altitudes. Sherpas are hired to do much of the difficult and dangerous work for an expedition. For example, they may plan the route and install a safety rope along it. They also place ladders across the deep cracks in the ice that are called crevasses.

The table shows the mass of supplies carried by 8 Sherpas. What is the mean weight carried by each of these Sherpas?

Paul solved the problem this way:

$$
\begin{array}{r}
27.2 \\
28.4 \\
26.5 \\
27.2 \\
29.1 \\
25.9 \\
25.7 \\
+\ 27.6 \\
\hline
217.6
\end{array}
$$

$$
\begin{array}{r}
272 \\
8)\overline{217.6}
\end{array}
$$

The average weight was 272 kilograms.

Weight Carried (kilograms)

27.2	29.1
28.4	25.9
26.5	25.7
27.2	27.6

Go back and look at the problem. Why doesn't Paul's answer make sense? Compare the mean Paul calculated to the numbers in the table.

Answer the questions. ◄ MOC 102, 274, 185

1. Would you expect the answer to be more than or less than 29.1 kilograms? Explain.

   _____

   _____

2. Did Paul make a mistake when he divided? _____

3. What did Paul do wrong? _____

4. What is the correct answer to the problem? _____

5. Is your answer between 25.7 and 29.1 kg? _____

   If you answered *no*, go back and try again.

Comparing your answer to a number or numbers from the problem can often give you an idea about whether an answer is reasonable. It can help you realize that you may have made a careless mistake or used the wrong operation.

Vocabulary ▼ mass

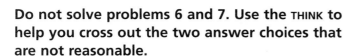

Do not solve problems 6 and 7. Use the THINK to help you cross out the two answer choices that are not reasonable.

6. The Khumbu Icefall glacier moves at a rate of about 3 feet per day. How many inches per minute is that? ◀ MOC 180

   THINK: Is the answer *greater than* or *less than* 3 inches per minute?

   _____

Between the Everest Base Camp and Camp I, the climbers must go through the Khumbu Icefall. This is a glacier that is shifting constantly. You can even hear the creaks and groans as it moves.

   A. 180 in. per min

   B. 0.04 in. per min

   C. 0.025 in. per min

   D. 25 in. per min

7. As you climb higher, the temperature drops. It falls an average of $3\frac{1}{2}°$F for every 1000 feet you climb. At that rate, if it's 11°F at Camp III, which is 24,000 feet above sea level, about how cold would it be at the summit? (**HINT:** You can find the altitude at the summit on page 75.) ◀ MOC 136

   THINK: Is the answer *greater than* or *less than* 11°F ? _____

   A. about ⁻20°F

   B. about 15°F

   C. about $⁻6\frac{1}{2}°$F

   D. about 21°F

Look back at exercises 6 and 7 to answer the questions.

8. How did you decide whether your answer to exercise 6 was *greater than* or *less than* 3 inches per minute?

   _____

   _____

   _____

9. How did you decide whether your answer to exercise 7 was *greater than* or *less than* 11°F?

   _____

   _____

   _____

more ▶

Ask yourself a question to help you decide whether an answer is reasonable.

Ken Noguchi, a Japanese graduate student, organized a Mount Everest clean-up expedition in 2000. The group collected about $1\frac{1}{2}$ tons of trash on the path above Base Camp.

Do not solve exercises 10–12. Use the THINK to help you cross out the two answer choices that are not reasonable.

10. Between 1953 and the mid-1990s, about 50 tons of plastic, glass, and metal were dumped on Mount Everest by climbing expeditions. About how many pounds of trash per year is that? ◄MOC 274, 536

    THINK: Is the answer *greater than* or *less than* 50 pounds per year? _____

    A. about $2\frac{1}{4}$ pounds per year

    B. about 22 pounds per year

    C. about 2500 pounds per year

    D. about 4000 pounds per year

11. In the mid-1990s, Nepal's government made new rules about leaving garbage on Mount Everest. In the previous 40 years, each expedition left behind an average of 805 pounds of oxygen bottles, tents, and other trash. About how many such expeditions would it take to account for 100,000 pounds of garbage? ◄MOC 180

    THINK: Is the answer *less than 800* or *between 800 and 100,000*? _____

    A. 1,242

    B. 1,160

    C. 124

    D. 116

80

12. Expeditions use yaks to help carry supplies to Base Camp. If each yak costs $50 and can carry 120 pounds, about how many yaks will be needed to carry 18,000 pounds of supplies for the group? ◂MOC 176–178

THINK: Will you need *more than* or *fewer than* 100 yaks? _____

A. 180   **C.** 5

B. 150   **D.** 3600

Look back at exercises 10–12 to answer the questions.

13. How did you decide whether your answer to exercise 10 should be *greater than* or *less than* 50 pounds per year?

_____

_____

_____

_____

14. How did you decide whether your answer to exercise 11 should be *less than 805* or *between 805 and 100,000*?

_____

_____

_____

_____

15. How did you decide whether your answer to exercise 12 should be *more than* or *fewer than* 100 yaks?

_____

_____

_____

_____

more ▶

When you estimate, use numbers that are easy to work with but still give you a good idea of the size of the answer.

As a climber goes higher, the air pressure decreases. The air seems to get thinner and it's harder to breathe because a person cannot take in as much oxygen. Because of the limited oxygen and the cold, altitudes above 26,000 feet are called the Death Zone. At high elevations, climbers often use oxygen bottles, which are actually tanks that are small enough to be carried and strong enough to contain oxygen at high pressure.

Follow the steps to rule out answer choices that are not reasonable.

16. One type of oxygen bottle is a cylinder 19 inches long and 4.25 inches in diameter. What is the volume of a cylinder this size?

Circle the best estimate of the _radius_ of the cylinder. ◀MOC 178, 370

A. 20 in.　　**B.** 4 in.　　**C.** 2 in.　　**D.** 1 in.

Circle the expression that gives the closest estimate of the volume of the cylinder in cubic inches. ◀MOC 413

A. (20)(4)　　**B.** (3)(2)²(20)　　**C.** 20 ÷ 4　　**D.** (3.14)(4)²(20)

What is your estimate of the volume? ◀MOC 158–159

About _____ cubic inches

Use your estimate to cross out two answer choices that are not reasonable.

A. 327 in.³　　**B.** 269 in.³　　**C.** 78 in.³　　**D.** 24.5 in.³

17. Climbers using bottled oxygen can set the rate at which the oxygen flows so that they get the right amount of extra oxygen. One kind of oxygen bottle will last about 6.5 hours if the flow rate is 2 liters per minute. About how many liters of oxygen are in the bottle?

Circle the expression that gives the best estimate of the amount of oxygen in the bottle.

A. (2)(7)　　**B.** $\frac{60}{6} \times 2$　　**C.** 6(2) ÷ 60　　**D.** $(60)(6\frac{1}{2})(2)$

What is your estimate for the amount of oxygen in the bottle? ◀MOC 149–150

About _____ liters

Use your estimate to cross out two answer choices that are not reasonable.

A. 20 liters　　**B.** 480 liters　　**C.** 780 liters　　**D.** 980 liters

82

18. Climbers need to know how long their bottled oxygen will last. The higher the flow rate, the sooner the bottle will be empty. About how many hours will the bottle from exercise 17 last if the flow rate is 2.75 liters per minute instead of 2 liters per minute?

Circle the proportion you could solve to give the closest estimate of the number of hours. ◀MOC 428

A. $\frac{3}{2} = \frac{x}{6}$ **C.** $\frac{2}{6} = \frac{x}{3}$

B. $\frac{2}{3} = \frac{x}{6}$ **D.** $\frac{x}{2} = \frac{3}{6}$

What is your estimate for the number of hours? ◀MOC 434

About _____ hours

Use your estimate to cross out two answer choices that are not reasonable.

A. 9.7 hours   **C.** 4.7 hours

B. 6.7 hours   **D.** 0.7 hours

---

19. Your expedition spent about $30,000 for sixty-five 1.1-kiloliter oxygen bottles to use at Camps III and IV and a reserve of 10 extra bottles. What was the cost per bottle?

Circle the expression that gives the best estimate of the cost per bottle. ◀MOC 179

A. $30,000 ÷ 65 × 1.1   **C.** 75 ÷ $30,000

B. $30,000 ÷ (65 + 10)   **D.** 1.1(65 + 10)

What is your estimate for the cost per bottle? About _____

Use your estimate to cross out two answer choices that are not reasonable.

A. $400   **C.** $450

B. $25,000   **D.** $20,065

After you solve a problem, look back to make sure your reasoning is correct.

On Sir Edmund Hillary's expedition, teams of 2 were formed for attempts to ascend to the summit from the final camp. Your expedition leader also plans to form teams of 2. There are 6 climbers that could try for the summit.

Problem How many different teams of 2 can be formed from a group of 6 climbers? ◀ MOC 480, 460

Tasha's Solution

Study the problem and Tasha's solution. Answer the questions below to decide whether her answer makes sense.

I made an organized list. I used the letters A–F for the 6 climbers.

AB	BA	CA	DA	EA	FA
AC	BC	CB	DB	EB	FB
AD	BD	CD	DC	EC	FC
AE	BE	CE	DE	ED	FD
AF	BF	CF	DF	EF	FE

30 different teams can be formed.

Answer the questions about Tasha's solution.

1. Was Tasha correct not to include teams represented by double letters, such as AA and BB? Explain.

_____

_____

2. Is team AB different from team BA? Explain.

_____

3. What was the mistake in Tasha's reasoning?

_____

_____

4. How can Tasha correct her reasoning?

_____

5. What is the correct answer?

_____

84

You ask a few members of the expedition to solve some problems for you. They do it late at night when they are tired and you find some errors in their reasoning.

Look back at each solution. Explain the error in reasoning and then give the correct answer.

6. The 2-person team plans to leave the camp at 6 A.M., climb to the summit, and return by 4 P.M. If climbers use a flow rate to make each bottle last 4 hours, how many bottles of oxygen should each climber take? (**HINT:** A calculation may be correct but you still have to interpret the result in a sensible way.) ◀MOC 182

Jack's Solution

6 A.M. to 4 P.M. is 10 hours
10 hours ÷ 4 hours = $2\frac{1}{2}$
Each climber should take
$2\frac{1}{2}$ bottles of oxygen.

Looking back at this solution, I see that _____

_____

Correct answer _____

---

7. What is the volume of the symmetrical tent shown in the diagram? ◀MOC 397, 408

Jane's Solution

I'll use the formula for volume of a triangular prism. B is the area of the triangular base and h is the height of the prism, which is the length of the tent.

$$V = Bh$$
$$= \frac{1}{2}(3)(3)(4)$$
$$= 18$$

The volume of the tent is 18 cubic feet.

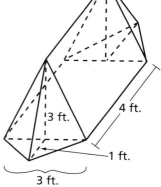

3 ft.

4 ft.

1 ft.

3 ft.

Jane did not include the volume of _____

_____

I would find the additional volume this way:

_____

_____

_____

Correct answer _____

more ▶

Vocabulary ▾ symmetrical ▾ triangular prism ▾ base of prism

Even the best mathematicians look back carefully at the thinking they used to solve a problem.

Look back at each solution. Explain the error in reasoning and then give the correct answer.

8. Otzi the Iceman died on a mountain in about 3300 B.C. About how old was his body when it was discovered in 1991? ◄MOC 136

Did you know?
Otzi the Iceman is the earliest known mountain explorer. Otzi's body was discovered when the glacier that preserved it melted. A backpack, a fur cloak, food, a bow and arrows, a flint knife, and a copper ax were found near him.

Jim's Solution
Round 1991 to 2000
3300 – 2000 = 1300
The body was about 1300 years old.

Looking back at Jim's solution, I see that _____

_____

_____

Correct answer _____

All of Mount Everest is above sea level but there are mountains where part of the mountain is below sea level. You want to talk about this in one of your reports.

9. Mauna Kea in Hawaii rises from the floor of the Pacific Ocean. The mountain rises 19,600 feet from the sea floor to sea level and it rises another 13,792 feet above sea level. What percent of the mountain's height is above sea level? ◄MOC 444

Joan's Solution
Fraction above water $= \frac{13,792}{19,600}$
Write as a decimal $\frac{13,792}{19,600} \approx 0.70$
About 70% of the mountain's height is above water.

Looking back at Joan's solution, I see that _____

_____

_____

Correct answer _____

10. You read that, at the top of Mount Everest one day, the temperature was ⁻31°F, or ⁻35°C. You notice that the number of degrees Fahrenheit is close to the number of degrees Celsius. At what temperature is the number of degrees the same in both scales? ◀ MOC 567, 239

Jon's Solution   I'll use the formula for converting degrees Celsius to degrees Fahrenheit:
$$F = \frac{9}{5}C + 32$$
I'll let x stand for the answer, the temperature at which the number of degrees is the same in both scales. This means that I can substitute x for both C and F in the formula.
$$x = \frac{9}{5}x + 32$$
To solve for x, I'll subtract $\frac{9}{5}x$.
$$x = \frac{9}{5}x - \frac{9}{5}x + 32$$
$$x = 32$$
So, 32°F and 32°C measure the same temperature.

Looking back at Jon's solution, I see that _____

_____

_____

Correct answer _____

Two of the team members have made it to the top of Mount Everest and have come down to Base Camp successfully. As everyone celebrates, you realize you would like to do this again.

11. You plan a return expedition for the year 2008. You decide to make it a long and patriotic ascent by beginning your trip from Kathmandu at noon on February 22, George Washington's birthday, and reaching the summit at noon on Memorial Day, which is May 26 that year. How many days is that?

Jesse's Solution

2/22 noon–2/28 noon	→	6 days
2/28 noon–3/1 noon	→	1 day
3/1 noon–3/31 noon	→	30 days
3/31 noon–4/1 noon	→	1 day
4/1 noon–5/1 noon	→	30 days
5/1 noon–5/26 noon	→	25 days
Total		93 days

Looking back at Jesse's solution, I see that _____

_____

_____

Correct answer _____

Fill in the circle with the letter of the correct answer.

1. A question asks for the price of a certain kind of cheese. Which of the following units would best be used with the answer?

   A ounces per pound

   B ounces per cubic centimeter

   C dollars per pound

   D holes per square inch

2. How many $15-CDs can you buy if you have $48.00?

   A 3

   B 3.2

   C $3\frac{3}{15}$

   D 4

3. Last week, the lowest noontime temperature was $^-3°F$ and the highest was $17°F$. Which of the following must be true about the mean noontime temperature for the week?

   A It is equal to or less than $^-3°F$.

   B It is between $^-3°F$ and $17°F$.

   C It is equal to or greater than $17°F$.

   D can't tell

4. A pool is 24 feet long, 15 feet wide, and 6 feet deep. Which unit is best for reporting the volume of the pool?

   A square feet

   B feet

   C cubic yards

   D all of these

5. The answer is 675 feet per minute. Which of these is most likely the question?

   A What is the surface area of the jet?

   B Which jet is traveling fastest?

   C How much shorter is the first jet?

   D At what rate is the jet descending?

Fill in the circle with the letter of the correct answer. Tell why you made your choice.

6. A cube is 3.1 cm long. What is the surface area of the cube? (HINT: Look for the most reasonable answer.)

   Ⓐ 57.7 cm² _____

   Ⓑ 18.6 cm² _____

   Ⓒ 127.1 cm² _____

   Ⓓ 29.8 cm² _____

For exercises 7–9, write the answer on the lines provided.

7. A team has won 78 games and lost 38 games. Write an expression that gives an estimate of the percent of its games that the team has won.

   _____

8. John started his bike trip at 10:30 A.M. By noon, he had biked 45 kilometers. If he continued at that rate, at what time did he reach his goal of 75 kilometers?

   _____

9. Show two ways that you can look back at your solution to problem 8 to check it.

   _____
   _____
   _____
   _____
   _____

BUILDING TO REMEMBER

Putting It All Together

HELP WANTED

Assistant to the director of a film on the Vietnam Veterans Memorial

(*The Wall*) in Washington, D. C.

Must have interest in history and desire to travel. Apply to Michael Ortega, Director.

In this chapter, you will learn about the tremendous effort it took to turn an idea into a national monument. You'll also see how the method used to solve math problems can be used for all sorts of problems, even problems that arise in making a film. You'll put together all the skills you've learned so far to see how the four-step problem-solving method (**Understand, Plan, Try, Look Back**) can help you become a better problem solver.

▼ This part of the Vietnam Veterans Memorial is often called *The Wall*. It recognizes those who lost their lives as a result of service in the Vietnam War with lists of their names organized by year.

▲ Visitors have left over 25,000 messages and gifts at The Wall. National Park Service Rangers collect these remembrances every day. Many of the objects left at The Wall have been put on display at the Smithsonian Institution in Washington, D. C.

▲ More than four million people visit the Vietnam Veterans Memorial annually.

Now it's time to apply what you've learned.

You applied for the job to be assistant to the director of the film on the Vietnam Veterans Memorial and you were chosen for the job. Now you want to learn about how the Memorial came to be.

You learn about one of the key people who made this happen, Maya Lin, the designer of The Wall. She and the veterans group funding the memorial had a big vision and went through many steps to make their vision a reality. They needed to understand what they wanted to accomplish, make a plan, implement their plan, and then review what they had done.

This is very similar to the problem-solving method you have been learning about in this book.

Maya Lin was a student at Yale University when her design for the Vietnam Veterans Memorial was selected from among 1421 entries into the design competition.

Turning a vision into a reality usually takes an organized approach. In mathematics, the four-step problem-solving method provides an organized approach to solving problems.

Step 1 ▸ **Understand** the problem.

Step 2 ▸ **Plan** how to solve the problem.

Step 3 ▸ **Try** to solve the problem.

Step 4 ▸ **Look Back** at your solution to check it.

You've already learned about each of these four steps in this book.

A name is being etched onto the Vietnam Veterans Memorial.

Name the problem-solving step or steps covered in each chapter of this book. Write a short summary of the problem-solving techniques you studied.

Chapter 1 _____

_____

Chapter 2 _____

_____

Chapter 3 _____

_____

Chapter 4 _____

_____

Chapter 5 _____

_____

Now it's time to put all four steps together.

Sometimes, the information you need is in a table, graph, or chart.

Michael Ortega, the director of the film, asks you to research the key events in the creation of the Vietnam Veterans Memorial Wall. This is the time line you created after doing some research.

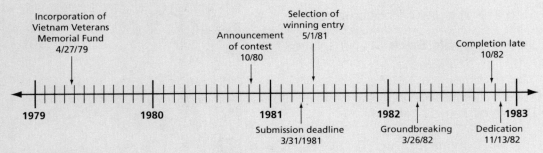

Problem More than 3 years passed between the time the Vietnam Veterans Memorial Fund was created and the dedication of The Wall. To the nearest 5%, what percent of the time from incorporation of the fund to completion of the Memorial was the construction phase?

Answer the questions to see how the four-step problem-solving method can be used to solve the problem above.

▸ **Understand**

1. What does the problem ask you to find?

_____

_____

2. Place a ✔ in the box if that information is needed to solve the problem.

☐ Construction began on March 26, 1982.

☐ 1980 was a leap year.

☐ The Vietnam Veterans Memorial was completed in late October of 1982.

▸ **Plan**

3. Circle the equation or equations you could use to find what percent a part is of a whole. ◂**MOC 444**

A. $\text{percent} = \frac{\text{whole}}{\text{part}} \times 100\%$

B. $\text{percent} = \frac{\text{part}}{\text{whole}} \times 100\%$

C. $\frac{\text{part}}{\text{whole}} = \frac{\text{percent}}{100}$

4. Write a plan that you could use to solve the problem.

   Plan

   _____

   _____

   _____

▶ Try

5. Show how you would carry out the plan.

6. Write a sentence that tells the solution to the problem.

   _____

   _____

▶ Look Back

7. Did you answer the question that was asked? _____

   If you answered *no*, go back and redo your work.

8. Did you round your answer to the nearest 5%? ◀ MOC 021 _____

   If you answered *no*, go back and round your answer.

9. Does the size of your answer make sense?

   _____

   If you answered *no*, go back and check your calculations
   and your reasoning.

Did you know?
The Vietnam Memorial Fund raised
nearly $9,000,000 through private
contributions. Federal funds were not
used to build The Wall.

more ▶

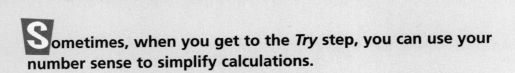

Sometimes, when you get to the *Try* step, you can use your number sense to simplify calculations.

On March 31, 1981, the deadline for submitting a design for the Memorial Contest, 1421 entries had been received. Of those entries, 232 made it to the second round of the selection process. Only 39 of those made it to the third and final round.

Problem You wonder whether it was harder to make it past the first round or the second. If the winning designs had been picked at random, which of these would have been more probable: an entry making it to the second round or an entry in the second round making it to the final round?

Answer the questions to see how the four-step problem-solving method can be used to solve the problem above.

▶ **Understand**

10. What does the problem ask you to find?

_____

_____

11. Place a ✔ in the box if that information is needed to solve the problem.

☐ The deadline for entries was March 31, 1981.

☐ There were 1421 entries in all.

☐ 232 entries made it to the second round and 39 of those made it to the final round.

▶ **Plan**

12. Fill in the blanks to complete the plan. ◀ MOC 465

- Write a fraction to show the probability of making it to the second round.

  Write _____ in the numerator and _____ in the denominator. _____.

- Write a fraction for the probability of a design in the second round making it to the third round.

  Write _____ in the numerator and _____ in the denominator. _____.

- Compare _____ and _____ to see which probability is greater.

96   Vocabulary ▾ random ▾ probability

▸ **Try**

13. To the nearest thousandth, find the decimal equivalents of your fractions.

_____

_____

14. Compare the decimal equivalents.

_____

15. Write a sentence that tells the solution to the problem.

_____

_____

▸ **Look Back**

16. Did you answer the question that was asked? _____

If you answered *no*, go back and redo your work.

17. Did you check your calculations? _____

If you answered *no*, go back and check them.

Did you know?

The design entries were displayed at an airport hangar at Andrews Air Force Base. It took more than 35,000 square feet of floor space to display the designs. Each design was given a number, so the judges didn't know who the entrants were. After they selected Number 1026 for first place, they found out that Maya Lin was the winner.

more ▸

Sometimes your plan may have many steps.

The director of the film wants you to get some financial information about the contest. Each of the 1421 entrants paid $20 to enter the contest. Of the 39 entries that made it to the final round of the contest, 15 received an honorable mention and $1000 each. An award of $5,000 was given to the third place design, $10,000 to the second place finisher, and $20,000 to Maya Lin for first place.

Problem With all that money given away to winners, how much more money was distributed in prizes than was received in entry fees?

Answer the questions to see how the four-step problem-solving method can be used to solve the problem above.

▸ **Understand**

18. What does the problem ask you to find?

_____

_____

_____

19. Place a ✔ in the box if that information is needed to solve the problem.

☐ Thirty-nine entries made it to the final round.

☐ Each person submitting an entry paid $20.

☐ The second place finisher received $10,000.

▸ **Plan**

20. Circle the expression that represents the difference between income and payout. ◀ MOC 204

   A. total collected in fees ÷ total paid out in prizes

   B. total collected in fees − total paid out in prizes

   C. total paid out in prizes − total collected in fees

21. Write a plan for solving the problem. ◂MOC 145

Plan

_____

_____

_____

_____

▸**Try**

22. Show how you would carry out the plan.

Maya Lin's winning design

23. Write a sentence that tells the solution to the problem.

_____

_____

▸**Look Back**

24. Did you answer the question that was asked? _____

If you answered *no*, go back and redo your work.

25. Is your prize-money sum more than the amount collected in fees? _____

If you answered *no*, go back and check your calculations.

more ▸

A diagram can often help you visualize and solve a problem.

The director of the film wants you to plan some of the shots that you will film before leaving for Washington, D. C. Panels are all the same width, but their heights vary.

Problem You are planning a scene in which the camera will slowly pan from panel 19E to panel 28W. To plan the shot, find the distance in feet along the Wall from the center of 19E to the center of 28W.

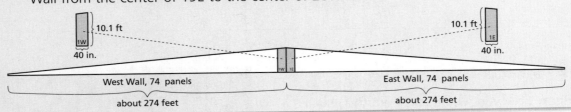

Answer the questions to see how the four-step problem-solving method can be used to solve the problem above.

▶ **Understand**

26. What does the problem ask you to find?

_____

27. Place a ✔ in the box if that information is needed to solve the problem.

☐ the width of each panel   ☐ the height of each panel

☐ the number of rows of names on each panel

28. If you left any boxes unchecked in exercise 27, explain why you don't need that information.

_____

_____

_____

▶ **Plan**

29. Write a plan that could be used to solve the problem.

Plan

_____

_____

_____

_____

100

 ▸**Try**

30. Show how you would carry out the plan. ◄MOC 145

31. Write a sentence that tells the solution to the problem.

_____

▸**Look Back**

32. Did you answer the question that was asked? _____

If you answered *no*, go back and redo your work.

33. Circle the expression whose value would best help you estimate your answer. ◄MOC 092, 145

A. $(30 - 20) \times (40 \div 10)$ **C.** $(30 + 20) \times (40 \div 10)$

B. $(70 - 20) \times 70 - (30 \div 40)$ **D.** $(20 + {}^-30) \times (40 \div 12)$

34. Use the expression you circled to estimate the answer.

_____

35. Does your estimate show that your answer is reasonable? _____

If you answered *no*, go back and check your work.

36. Does your answer have the correct unit? _____

If you answered *no*, go back and add or change the unit.

When solving problems on your own, you can always use the four-step method.

It won't solve the problem for you, but it can help you keep organized. Here are some questions to think about as you use this method.

▶ Understand

- Do I know what each word in the problem means? (If you don't know what a word means, use *Math on Call*, the Vocabulary section of this book, your math book, or a dictionary to help you.)
- What information do I have?
- What do I need to find out?
- Should my answer be an estimate or an exact number?
- Can I draw a diagram to help me understand the problem?
- Is there any information that is missing? If so, can I find it?
- Is there extra information that I should ignore?

▶ Plan

- Can I draw a diagram to help me solve the problem?
- Can I write an expression or equation that shows what the problem says?
- Can I use a formula?
- Do I need to compute more than once?

▶ Try

- Am I carrying out each step of my plan?
- Am I using the correct information from the problem?
- Am I computing correctly?
- Is my plan working, or do I need to change it?

▶ Look Back

- Did I answer the question that was asked?
- Did I label my answer correctly?
- Can I check whether my answer makes sense by comparing it to one of the other numbers in the problem?
- Can I use estimation to check whether my answer is reasonable?
- Does the reasoning I used make sense?

Solve the problem. Explain how you used each of the four problem-solving steps. Use the questions on page 102 to help you.

1. You are planning a dolly shot in which the camera will move along a straight track from one tip of the memorial to the other. To build the track for the dolly shot you need to know that distance. How many meters is it from one tip straight across to the other? ◀ MOC 359

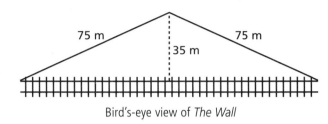

75 m   35 m   75 m

Bird's-eye view of *The Wall*

▶ **Understand**

_____

_____

_____

▶ **Plan**

_____

_____

▶ **Try**

Answer in a complete sentence.

_____

▶ **Look Back**

_____

_____

_____

_____

more ▶

Use everything you've learned so far to solve the problems.

While you are in Washington, D. C., you want to visit other memorials and monuments. First on your list is the Washington Monument. You find a map that shows the location of some of the monuments and memorials in Washington, D. C.

Solve the problems. Explain how you used each of the four problem-solving steps. Use the questions on pages 102 to help you.

2. Based on the map, how far is it from the center of the Vietnam Veterans Memorial Wall to the Washington Monument? ◄ MOC 377

▸ **Understand**

_____

_____

▸ **Plan**

_____

_____

_____

▸ **Try**

Answer in a complete sentence.

_____

▸ **Look Back**

_____

_____

_____

_____

3. You decide to visit these five other memorials and museums: Korean War Veterans Memorial, U. S. Holocaust Memorial Museum, Thomas Jefferson Memorial, Vietnam Women's Memorial, John Paul Jones Memorial. In how many different orders might you visit these five places? ◂MOC 458–459

▸ Understand

_____

_____

_____

▸ Plan

_____

_____

_____

_____

▸ Try

Answer in a **complete sentence.**

_____

▸ Look Back

_____

_____

_____

_____

_____

Now you know how to use the four-step problem-solving method. You can use it whenever you solve math problems. You may want to keep this book handy, so that you can use the questions on page 102 to help you.

Good luck and have fun solving problems!

Exercises 1–7 are about this problem.

To go from New City to Paxton, you can take one straight road, or you can take highway 110 south 8 miles to Dellport and then take Highway 50 west 12 miles to Paxton. If you are going from New City to Paxton, the second route is longer. Write the difference in trip lengths as a percent of the shorter route. Round your answer to the nearest percent.

For exercises 1–3, fill in the circle with the letter of the correct answer.

1. Which information from the problem is *not* needed to solve the problem?

   (A) Dellport is south of New City.

   (B) The numbers of the two highways have a sum of 160.

   (C) Paxton is 12 miles from Dellport.

2. Which relationship is *least* helpful for solving the problem?

   (A) square of one leg + square of other leg = square of hypotenuse

   (B) sum of measures of angles of a triangle = 180°

   (C) percent increase = $\frac{\text{final} - \text{original}}{\text{original}}$

3. Write a plan that you could use for solving the problem.
   (**HINT:** A diagram might be useful.)

   Plan

   _____

   _____

   _____

4. Carry out the plan from exercise 3.

5. Write a sentence that gives the correct answer to the original problem. Be sure to include a label with the number.

_____

6. Explain how you could use estimation to check that your answer makes sense.

7. What are the four problem-solving steps? Choose one of the steps. Tell why you think that step was important in solving the problem on page 106.

_____

_____

_____

_____

_____

A acre

average

approximately

B bar graph

area

base of prism

circle graph

chord

circle

circumference

congruent

cubic inch (in.³)

counting numbers

cylinder

cubic foot (ft³)

D degrees (°) and minutes (')
of latitude

degrees (°) and minutes (')
of longitude

denominator

degrees Celsius (°C)

diameter

degrees Fahrenheit (°F)

difference

E elevation

estimation

equation

expression

equivalent

F feet per second

fewer

formula

function

H height

hypotenuse

I isosceles

L leap year

M mass

leg

maximum

line graph

mean

numerator

miles per hour (mph)

odd number

net

operation

percent (%)

origin

perimeter

P **Pacific Standard Time**

pi (π)

power

product

prime

proportion

probability

Pythagorean Theorem

Q quotient

range

R radius

ratio

random

ray

rectangle

scale on a map

rectangular prism

sector

regular

similar

square

slant height

square kilometer (km^2)

square mile (mi^2)

square pyramid

surface area

sum

survey

supplementary angle

symbol

symmetrical

trapezoid

table

tree diagram

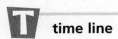 time line

triangular prism

truncated

 variable

volume

 whole number